No. 7220

Ideal School Supply Company

Grades 1-8

Math Card Games

Walter E. Rucker
Clyde A. Dilley

MATH CARD GAMES

Cover design by Christine Breves

Alsip, IL, 60482
Printed in U.S.A.

ISBN: 1-56451-061-1

6 7 8 9 10. 9 7

TABLE OF CONTENTS

TABLE OF CONTENTS

COMPUTATION (continued)

INTRODUCTION

There are two distinct purposes to the games in this book. First, each game provides practice using some mathematic concept or skill such as, counting, basic addition facts, the multiplication algorithm, and matching congruent figures. Second, each game also provides an opportunity for children to develop higher level thought processes such as, making and testing hypotheses and organizing data.

DRILL

Once children have developed an understanding of a mathematics concept or skill, they are ready to practice using that concept or skill to assimilate it and to develop efficiency and speed. Drill activity that is enjoyable to children, that they are anxious to complete, is most effective. Since most children love games, especially those they win, games that allow the player to use and develop mathematics skills are valuable classroom activities.

It must be remembered that these games can not be used to introduce or explain concepts or skills for which they provide practice. For example, a student must understand what addition is, and have a way of finding sums for combinations, before playing a game that provides practice in basic addition combinations.

HIGHER LEVEL PROCESSES

Although each game involves more than pure memory work or pure luck, both are factors in these games. But, in attempts to control their own destinies, maximizing the effects of good luck and minimizing the effects of bad luck, the students develop higher level thought processes. They begin to think in probabilistic terms (What can happen? What is most likely to happen?) and to develop strategies (hypotheses) to take advantage of the most likely happenings. They collect data from the results of their strategies and, when necessary, revise those strategies. Students usually discover that it is helpful to remember what cards have been played, what cards other players may have in their hands, or the positions of cards. They then develop techniques for organizing what they wish to remember to simplify the task.

These processes must be developed by the student alone. It does little good for teachers to talk at students about strategies or ways of organizing data. What the teacher must do is suggest, at the proper time, that strategies exist and that students may do better if they remember what cards have been played.

TEACHING THE GAMES

Introduce the games to a small group of students. Play with them or watch them play to be sure that all students understand all of the rules. Once some students understand a game, they can teach it to other students. Older students can probably read and understand, by themselves, the instructions to many games.

We suggest designating one section of the classroom a Game Corner where a variety of games are available for children to use in their free time or during regularly scheduled game periods.

Finally, we suggest that teachers encourage students to invent their own card games. They can invent games for themselves or for younger children. In addition to providing more games, this activity provides an opportunity for children to express their creativity. The creators of games probably learn more than do the players of the games.

MATERIALS

The cards needed for each game are described before the rules for each game. Teachers and students can easily make them from index cards, pieces of tag board cut into card-sized rectangles, or blank playing cards. Nylon felt-tipped pens or markers can be used to write on the cards but care must be taken to avoid color seepage to the reverse side.

For most games, cards and pencil and paper for score keeping are the only materials that are needed. However, four games call for additional materials. *Turn-down* uses a pair of dice. These can be made from regular wood blocks or from hexagonal pencils, by writing the numerals from 1–6 on the sides. *Order* uses a wood or styrofoam card holder described in the materials section for that game. In the geometry section, a yard stick and a meter stick are needed.

ATTRIBUTES

MAJOR CONCEPT: Attributes of figures

NUMBER OF PLAYERS: Two to four

MATERIALS: Thirty-two cards in sets of four. In each set, the figures on the cards are the same size and the same shape but they are different colors: one green, one red, one blue, and one yellow. Below are drawings of the eight figures.

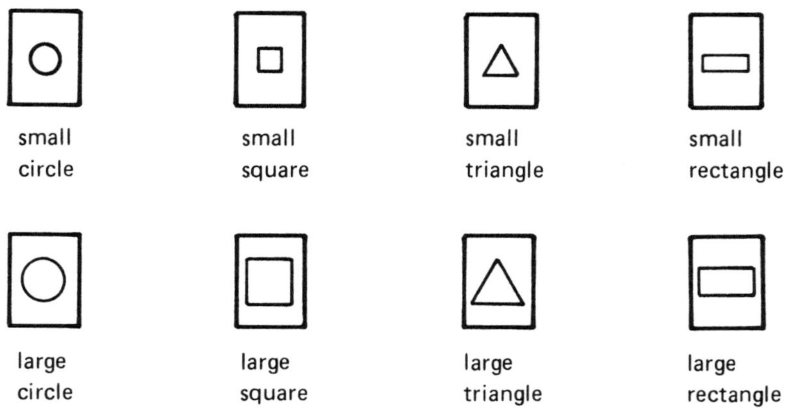

For example, the deck has four cards with small circles: one green, one red, one blue, and one yellow. Each figure has three attributes, color, shape, and size.

RULES: The dealer shuffles the deck and deals three cards, face-up, to each player. The next card is turned face-up in the center of the table and the remainder of the deck is placed face-down where all players can reach it.

The players build a row of figures, extending to the right of the first face-up figure. Each figure differs from the one on its left in exactly one attribute.

Sample row:

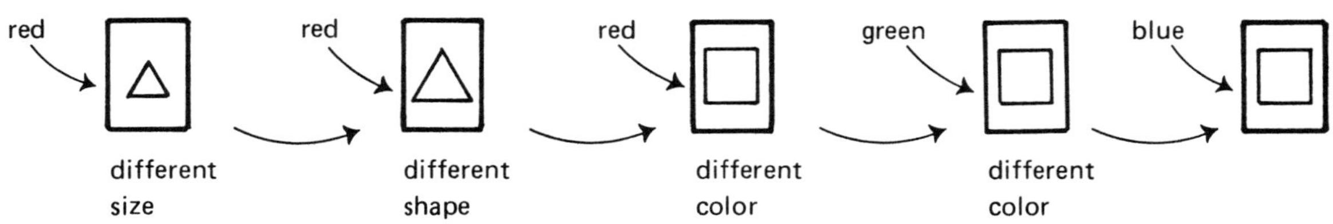

The player to the left of the dealer is the first player. If he has a figure that differs from the one turned up by the dealer in exactly one attribute, he places it face-up to the right of that card and the play passes to the player to the left. That player must play a figure that differs from the one played by the last player in exactly one attribute. If a player does not have a card to play, that player takes the top card from the deck and the play passes to the left. The first player to run out of cards is the winner.

VARIATIONS: Instead of building a row of figures that differ from their neighbors in exactly one attribute, the players can build a row of figures that differ from their neighbors in exactly two ways or exactly three ways.

The deck can be changed, also, by increasing the number of attributes of each figure. For example, another thirty-two cards can be made that are similar to the thirty-two cards described above except that the interiors of the figures are also colored. When all sixty-four cards are put together, each figure has four attributes, shape, size, color, and interior. Then the game can involve building rows of figures differing in exactly one, two, three, or four attributes.

SNAKE (Counting)

MAJOR CONCEPT: Matching sets and numerals

NUMBER OF PLAYERS: Two or more

MATERIALS: One each of the cards in this set:

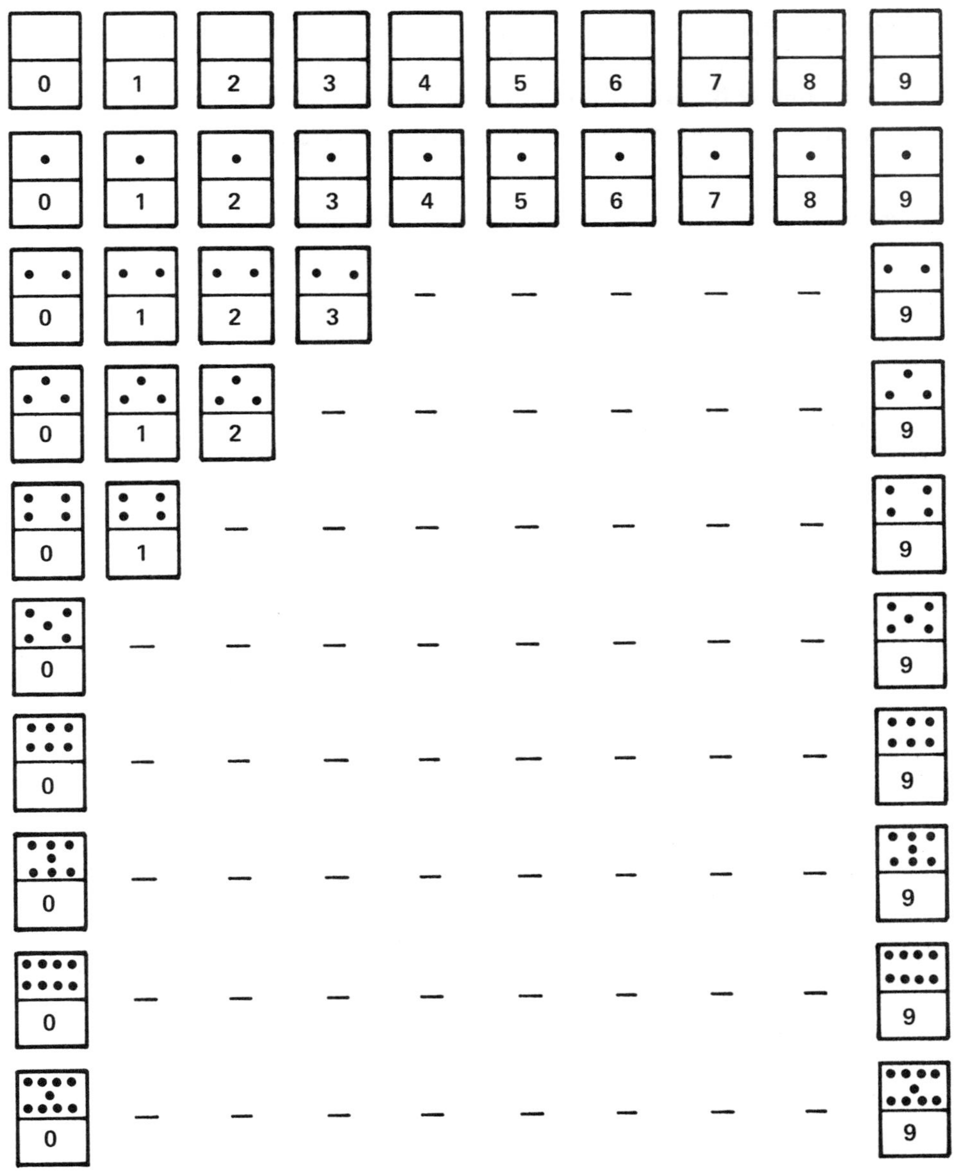

RULES: The dealer shuffles the deck and deals each player three cards face-up. She places the rest of the deck face-up in front of her. At this point, the distribution looks like this:

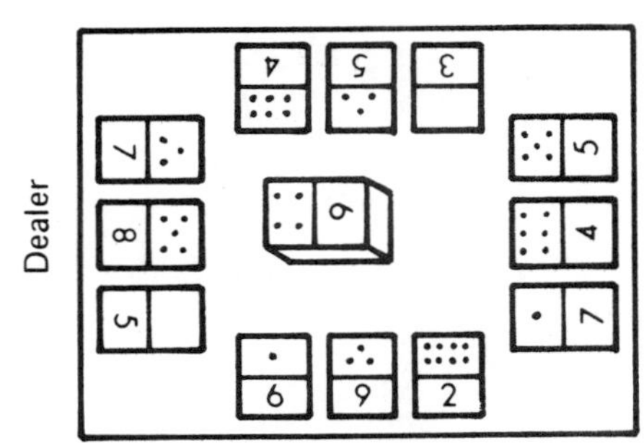

Starting with the player to the left of the dealer, each player in turn checks her cards for *doubles*. A *double* is a card on which the numeral represents the number of dots:

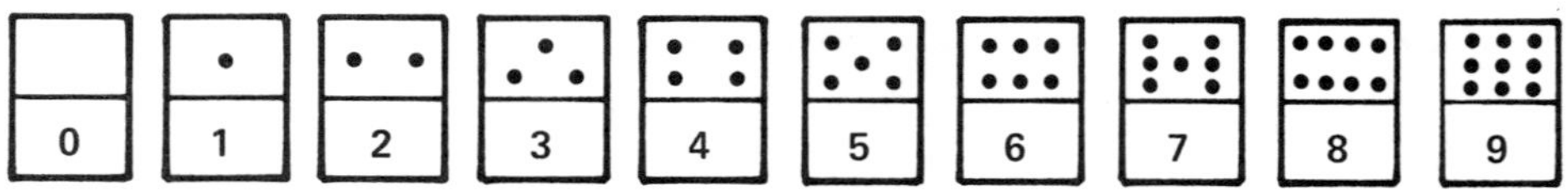

The first player to have a double places it face-up in the center of the table. If no player has a double, each player in turn draws the top card from the deck until a double is drawn. Each player collects the *non-double* cards that she draws.

After the first double has been played, the next player looks at her cards for one with a numeral that matches the dot half of the first double or a card with dots to match the numeral half of the first double.

Sample play:

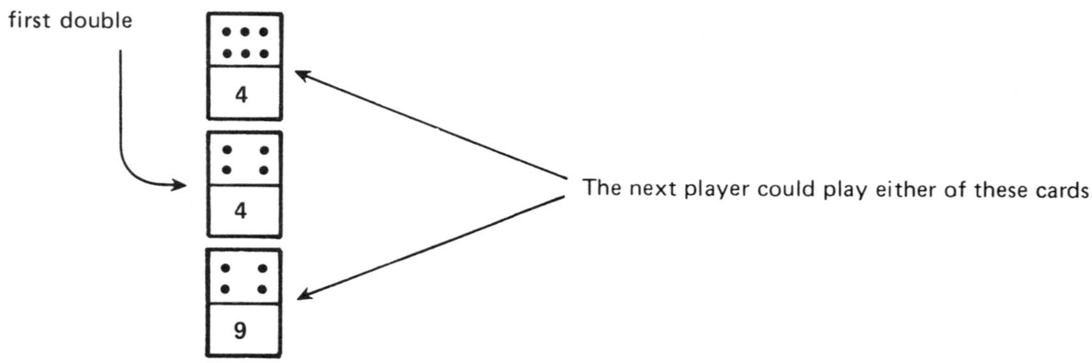

If she can not match the first double, the player must draw the top card from the deck and place it face-up in front of her. When other doubles are played, they must be placed horizontally so they are open for play on both ends.

Sample play:

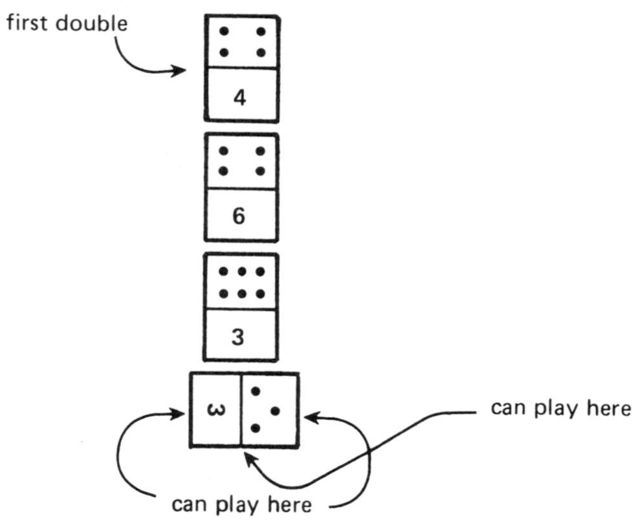

Play continues in the above manner until a player plays all of her cards. She is the winner.

BUILD-A-BOOK

MAJOR CONCEPT: Number-numeral recognition

NUMBER OF PLAYERS: Two or three

MATERIALS: One each of the following cards:

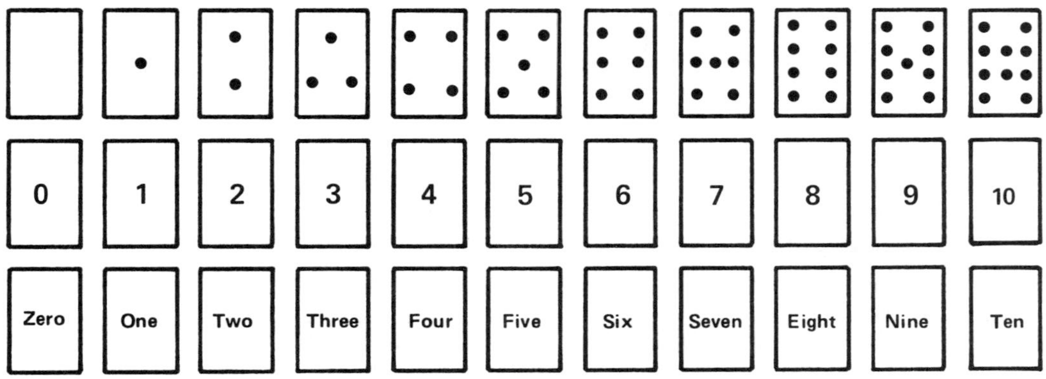

RULES: The dealer shuffles the cards and deals six cards face-down to each player. The next card is placed face-up in the center of the table to start a discard pile. The rest of the deck is placed face-down alongside of it. Each player holds her cards so that only she can see them. The object of the game is to build two books, each containing three cards that match.

Sample books:

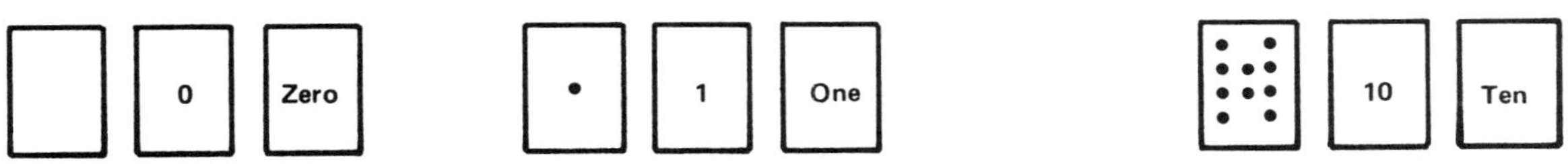

If the first player to the left of the dealer has two books, she puts both books on the table and wins the game. If not, she draws either the face-up card or the top card of the face-down deck. The player discards one card, face-up on the discard pile. Players take turns drawing and discarding until a person displays two books. That player is the winner.

WAR

MAJOR CONCEPT: Comparing numbers

NUMBER OF PLAYERS: Two to four

MATERIALS: Four each of the following cards:

0	1	2	3	4	5	6	7	8	9

RULES: One player shuffles the deck carefully and then deals an equal number of cards, face-down, to each player. Extra cards, when there are three players, are placed in the center of the table to be won by the winner of the first play. The players do not look at their cards, but leave the pile neatly stacked, face-down, in front of them.

Each player turns his top card face-up. The player with the greatest number wins the round and collects all of the face-up cards, and places them at the bottom of his pile. If there is a tie for the greatest number, the players that tied each turn up another card. The player with the greatest number wins and collects all of the face-up cards. This play is repeated until one player wins all of the cards, or until a predetermined time limit, of 5 to 15 minutes, expires. A player is eliminated from the game when he loses all of his cards.

ARITHMETIC MATCH

VARIATION 1: Addition Match

MAJOR CONCEPT: Basic addition facts

NUMBER OF PLAYERS: Two to six

MATERIALS: A deck of paired cards and one single card. One card of each pair shows a basic addition combination. The other card of the pair shows the sum.

Sample Cards:

3 + 6	9	3 + 2	5
5 + 4	9	4 + 8	12

The one unmatched card is the *square.*

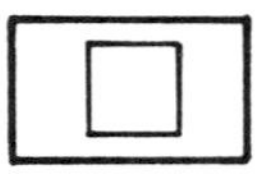

The number of cards in a deck will vary with the number of addition combinations to be practiced.

RULES: This game is played like *Old Maid.* The players sit in a circle. One player shuffles the cards and deals them, one at a time, face-down to the players. Some players may have one more card than the other players, but this is not important.

Each player picks up her cards and discards pairs that match; that is, one combination card and its sum card. Pairs are displayed, face-up, in front of the player so that the other players can check for errors.

Only pairs may be discarded. Regardless of how many cards a player has with the same sum, only one combination card and one sum card can be discarded in a single play. When this has been completed, each player has in her hand only unmatched cards.

Next the dealer takes, without looking, one card from the hand of the player on her right. If that card matches a card in her hand, she pairs the two cards and discards the pair face-up in front of her. Then the player on the dealer's right takes a card from the player on her right and, if possible, pairs it with one of her own hand.

Play continues in this manner around the circle. As the cards move from one player to another they will eventually all be paired and discarded — all, that is, but the *square* card. When a player loses all of her cards she is a winner and drops out of play. The loser is the last player left, the one who last holds the *square* card.

VARIATION 2: Subtraction Match

MAJOR CONCEPT: Basic subtraction facts

NUMBER OF PLAYERS: Two to six

This game is played in a way similar to Addition Match, but uses subtraction combination cards.

Sample cards:

9 – 2	7	17 – 9	8
5 – 5	0	12 – 5	7

VARIATION 3: Multiplication Match

MAJOR CONCEPT: Basic multiplication facts

NUMBER OF PLAYERS: Two to six

This game is played in a way similar to Addition Match, but uses multiplication combination cards.

Sample cards:

5 x 7	35

VARIATION 4: Division Match

MAJOR CONCEPT: Basic division facts

NUMBER OF PLAYERS: Two to six

This game is played in a way similar to Addition Match, but uses division combination cards.

Sample cards:

48 ÷ 8	6

ARITHMETIC CONCENTRATION

VARIATION 1: Addition Concentration

MAJOR CONCEPT: Basic addition facts

NUMBER OF PLAYERS: Two to four

MATERIALS: Twenty cards in pairs as follows:

2 + 8	8 + 7	5 + 6	9 + 7	8 + 4
7 + 3	9 + 6	8 + 3	8 + 8	5 + 7
7 + 6	8 + 6	4 + 3	5 + 4	2 + 6
9 + 4	9 + 5	2 + 5	3 + 6	5 + 3

RULES: Shuffle the cards carefully and deal them face-down into four rows with five cards in each row as shown.

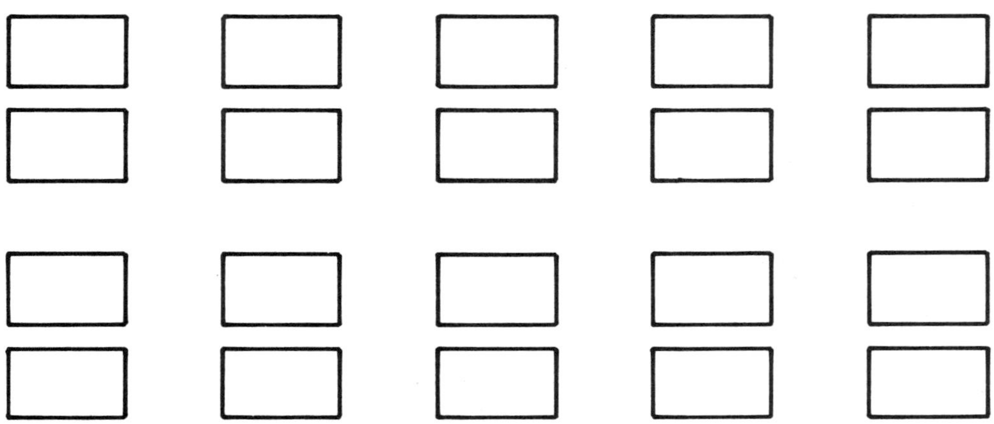

The player to the left of the dealer turns any two of the cards face-up in place. If the two cards have the same sum, the player takes them and places them face-down in front of her. She then plays again. If the cards do not have the same sum, they are turned back face-down in the same places. Players take turns, moving to the left. The game ends when all of the cards have been paired. The winner is the player with the most cards.

Obviously, the players who pay attention and remember the placements of the exposed cards have an advantage.

The deck of cards can be varied by changing combinations on the cards. For example, [2 + 9] in one game, and [7 + 4] for the sum 11, in another game. Also, the number of cards used can be varied.

VARIATION 2: Subtraction Concentration

MAJOR CONCEPT: Basic subtraction facts

NUMBER OF PLAYERS: Two to four

This game is played in a way similar to Addition Concentration, but uses subtraction cards.

Sample cards:

12 – 9	15 – 7
9 – 6	12 – 4

VARIATION 3: Multiplication Concentration

MAJOR CONCEPT: Basic multiplication facts

NUMBER OF PLAYERS: Two to four

MATERIALS: Ten pairs of cards based on the same principle as the following sample cards.

Sample cards:

7 x 8	56	6 x 7	42
9 x 5	45	9 x 3	27

RULES: This game is played in a way similar to Addition Concentration but uses multiplication cards.

VARIATION 4: Division Concentration

MAJOR CONCEPT: Basic division facts

NUMBER OF PLAYERS: Two to four

MATERIALS: Ten pairs of cards in which the two cards in a pair express the same quotient.

Sample cards:

81 ÷ 9	56 ÷ 7	63 ÷ 9	36 ÷ 6	45 ÷ 9
54 ÷ 6	32 ÷ 4	42 ÷ 6	48 ÷ 8	30 ÷ 6
36 ÷ 9	21 ÷ 7	18 ÷ 9	8 ÷ 8	0 ÷ 4
28 ÷ 7	18 ÷ 6	12 ÷ 6	7 ÷ 7	0 ÷ 9

This game is played in a way similar to Addition Concentration but uses division cards.

SLAPPING

VARIATION 1: Addition Slapping

MAJOR CONCEPT: Basic addition facts

NUMBER OF PLAYERS: Two

MATERIALS: Twelve sets of four cards. In each set the four cards show basic addition combinations for the same sum.

Sample cards:

a set for 7:	3 + 4	2 + 5	7 + 0	1 + 6
a set for 10:	4 + 6	2 + 8	9 + 1	5 + 5

RULES: Before play starts the players agree on the sum that will be the key number. For example, they might agree that 7 will be the key number. The deck is shuffled and completely dealt face-down into two stacks, one in front of each player. At the same time, both players turn the top cards of their stacks face-up, next to each other, in the center of the table. If the sum on one of the cards is the key number, 7 in this example, the players try to slap their hands down on top of that card. The first player to cover the card with his hand wins the round and collects the face-up cards which he puts at the bottom of his stack. The game continues with players turning cards one after the other, face-up, in the center of the table until the key sum appears. Once again, the first player to slap his hand on top of the key sum card wins all of the face-up cards and puts them at the bottom of his stack.

The play ends when one player loses all of his cards or when a predetermined time has expired. The player with the greater number of cards is the winner.

This game can be varied by using subtraction cards, division cards, or by mixing addition, subtraction, and division cards.

VARIATION 2: Slapping Number Pairs

MAJOR CONCEPT: Basic facts

NUMBER OF PLAYERS: Two

MATERIALS: One each of the following cards:

1 1								
2 1	2 2							
3 1	3 2	3 3						
4 1	4 2	4 3	4 4					
5 1	5 2	5 3	5 4	5 5				
6 1	6 2	6 3	6 4	6 5	6 6			
7 1	7 2	7 3	7 4	7 5	7 6	7 7		
8 1	8 2	8 3	8 4	8 5	8 6	8 7	8 8	
9 1	9 2	9 3	9 4	9 5	9 6	9 7	9 8	9 9

Several numbers are associated with each card: the sum, the difference, the product, and the quotient of the two numbers on the card. For example, the numbers associated with [8 / 2] are:

10 because $8 + 2 = 10$
6 because $8 - 2 = 6$
16 because $8 \times 2 = 16$
and 4 because $8 \div 2 = 4$

Notice that the *top* number of the card is used first and the *bottom* number is used second.

The numbers associated with [7 / 3] are

10 because 7 + 3 = 10
4 because 7 − 3 = 4
21 because 7 x 3 = 21
and $2\frac{1}{3}$ because 7 ÷ 3 = $2\frac{1}{3}$

RULES: This game is played in a way similar to Addition Slapping, except the players must compute all of the numbers associated with each card to see if the key number has been turned up. For example, if the key number is 10, the players should try to slap their hands on these cards.

[7 / 3] because 7 + 3 = 10

[5 / 2] because 5 x 2 = 10

[8 / 2] because 8 + 2 = 10

If the key number is 4, here are some of the cards that should be slapped.

[8 / 2] because 8 ÷ 2 = 4

[2 / 2] because 2 + 2 = 4

[6 / 2] because 6 − 2 = 4

ARITHMETIC WAR

VARIATION 1: Addition War

MAJOR CONCEPT: Basic addition facts

NUMBER OF PLAYERS: Two to four

MATERIALS: Four each of the following:

0	1	2	3	4	5	6	7	8	9

RULES: One player shuffles the deck carefully and then deals the cards one at a time, face-down, so that all players have the same number of cards. Extra cards, when there are three players, are placed in the center of the table to be won by the winner of the first play. The players do not look at their cards, but leave them face-down in piles.

The object of the game is to win as many cards as possible from the other players. The game ends when one player has all of the cards, or, if that does not happen, when a predetermined time limit expires. A reasonable time limit is from five to 15 minutes. A player is eliminated from the game when she loses all of her cards, or when she loses all but her last card. In the latter case, the last card is withdrawn from play.

To play the game, each player turns face-up the top two cards of her pile and announces the sum of the numbers on those cards for all to hear. The player with the greatest sum wins the round and collects as her prize all of the face-up cards which she places at the bottom of her pile. If there is a tie for the greatest sum, the players who tied have a play-off. They each turn, face-up, two more cards from their piles and announce the sums. The one with the greatest sum wins the play-off and collects all face-up cards from the regular round and the play-off. The players continue to play rounds as described above until a game winner is declared.

Players will sometimes make errors calculating sums. Therefore, they may challenge each other when they think that an incorrect sum has been announced. A player who wishes to challenge says, "challenge" and then announces what she thinks to be the correct sum. If that player is correct in her challenge, the player who first announced the incorrect sum automatically loses the round. If, however, the challenger is incorrect, she loses the round. If the challenged player or the challenger is not the winner of the hand, the loser of the challenge pays a penalty of two cards to the winner of the challenge.

VARIATION 2: Multiplication War

MAJOR CONCEPT: Basic multiplication facts

NUMBER OF PLAYERS: Two to four

MATERIALS: Same as Variation 1

RULES: This game is played in a way similar to Addition War but players announce the products of the cards turned face-up.

FISHIN'

VARIATION 1: Addition Fishin'

MAJOR CONCEPT: Basic addition facts

NUMBER OF PLAYERS: Two to six

MATERIALS: Twelve sets of four cards. Each of the four cards in a set has a basic combination for the same sum. Here are examples of some possible sets.

A set for 6:	4 + 2	5 + 1	6 + 0	3 + 3
A set for 10:	7 + 3	5 + 5	4 + 6	2 + 8
A set for 12:	3 + 9	8 + 4	7 + 5	6 + 6
A set for 15:	8 + 7	7 + 8	10 + 5	9 + 6
A set for 4:	2 + 2	3 + 1	1 + 3	0 + 4

RULES: One player shuffles the cards, deals five cards to each player, and places the rest of the deck face-down in the center of the table. Each player then discards *pairs* of matching cards. A pair is two cards from the same set. Each discarded pair is shown to the other players so they can check for errors. After all matching pairs have been discarded, play begins.

Play starts with the player to the left of the dealer and moves to the left. When it is his turn, a player asks the player on his right for a card with a specific sum. For example, he may say, "Give me a 6," or "Give me an 11." If the player who is asked has such a card, he must give it to the player who asked for it. If the asked player does not have such a card, then the player who asked takes a card from the deck. In either case, if pairs are formed, they are shown and discarded. The first player to run out of cards is the winner. Notice that it is possible for two players to tie, if they both run out of cards on the same play.

VARIATION 2: Subtraction Fishin'

MAJOR CONCEPT: Subtraction facts

NUMBER OF PLAYERS: Two to six

MATERIALS: Twelve sets of four cards. Each of the four cards in a set has a combination for the same difference. There should be sets resulting in differences from 0 –11. Here are some sample sets.

A set for 5:	8 – 3	12 – 7	6 – 1	15 – 10
A set for 9:	18 – 9	17 – 8	15 – 6	12 – 3
A set for 11:	11 – 0	12 – 1	14 – 3	17 – 6

RULES: This game is played in a way similar to Addition Fishin' but uses subtraction cards.

VARIATION 3: Division Fishin'

MAJOR CONCEPTS: Division facts

NUMBER OF PLAYERS: Two to six

MATERIALS: Twelve sets of four division cards. Each of the four cards in a set has a quotient between 0 –11. Here are some sample sets.

A set for 6:	48 ÷ 8	36 ÷ 6	24 ÷ 4	54 ÷ 9
A set for 0:	0 ÷ 4	0 ÷ 7	0 ÷ 5	0 ÷ 9
A set for 11:	88 ÷ 8	22 ÷ 2	33 ÷ 3	11 ÷ 1

RULES: This game is played in a way similar to Addition Fishin' but uses division cards.

PICK—UP

VARIATION 1: Addition Pick-Up

MAJOR CONCEPT: Basic addition facts

NUMBER OF PLAYERS: Two or more

MATERIALS: Two decks of the basic addition combinations, 0 + 0 through 9 + 9, with sums on the reverse side.

The sum, 10, is on the back.

RULES: A player shuffles one of the decks and deals three cards, with the sum-sides up, to each player. The rest of the deck is placed sum-side up in the center of the table.

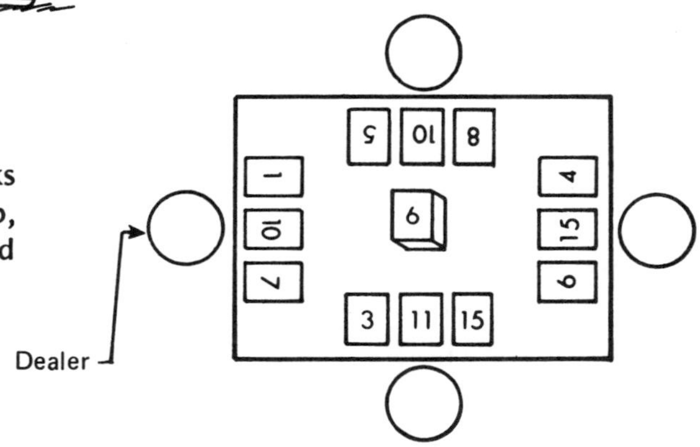

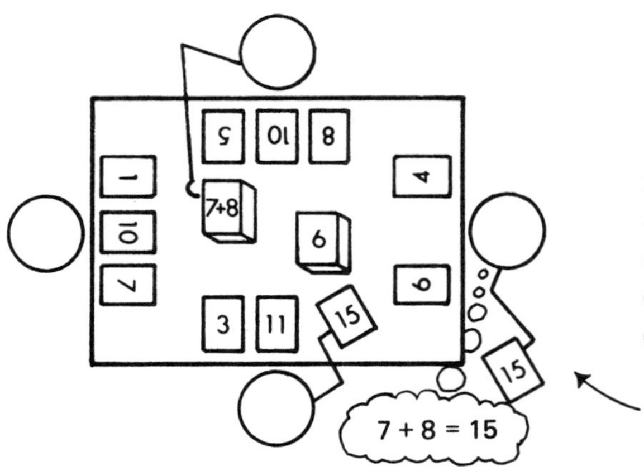

Next, the dealer shuffles the other deck and places it problem-side up directly in front of her. Each player with the sum of the top combination in front of her, picks up her sum card, shows it to the other players so that they can check, and then holds it in her hand.

Starting with the player to the left of the dealer, each sum card that was picked up is replaced by another sum card from the deck in the center of the table, so that each player again has three cards in front of her. Next, the dealer places the top combination on the bottom of the deck and play continues. The game ends when a player picks up her last sum card. The player holding the greatest number of cards wins the game.

VARIATION 2: Subtraction Pick-Up

MAJOR CONCEPT: Basic subtraction facts

NUMBER OF PLAYERS: Two or more

MATERIALS: Two decks of the basic division facts, 0 ÷ 1 through 81 ÷ 9, with quotients on the reverse side.

Sample cards:

0 – 0	1 – 0	1 – 1	- - - - - - - - - - - - - -	18 – 9

RULES: This game is played in a similar way to Addition Pick-Up but uses subtraction cards. One deck is used as a difference-deck and is placed in the center of the table. The other deck is used as a combination-deck and is placed in front of the dealer.

VARIATION 3: Multiplication Pick-Up

MAJOR CONCEPT: Basic multiplication facts

NUMBER OF PLAYERS: Two or more

MATERIALS: Two decks of the basic multiplication facts, 0 x 0 through 9 x 9, with products on the reverse side.

Sample cards:

0 x 0	0 x 1	- - - - - - - - - - - - - -	9 x 8	9 x 9

RULES: Multiplication Pick-Up is played in a similar way to Addition Pick-Up but uses multiplication cards. One deck is used as a product-deck and is placed in the center of the table. The other deck is used as a combination-deck and is placed in front of the dealer.

VARIATION 4: Division Pick-Up

MAJOR CONCEPT: Basic division facts

NUMBER OF PLAYERS: Two or more

MATERIALS: Two decks of the basic division facts, 0 ÷ 1 through 81 ÷ 9, with quotients on the reverse side.

Sample cards:

0 ÷ 1	0 ÷ 2	- - - - - - - - - - - - - -	72 ÷ 9	81 ÷ 9

RULES: This game is played in a similar way to Addition Pick-Up but uses division cards. One deck is used as a quotient-deck and is placed in the center of the table. The other deck is used as a combination-deck and is placed in front of the dealer.

TURN—DOWN

VARIATION 1: Factor Turn-Down

MAJOR CONCEPT: Factors of numbers 1 through 50

NUMBER OF PLAYERS: Two or more

MATERIALS: 1. Four each of the following digit cards:

1	2	3	4	5	6	7	8	9

2. The whole numbers from 1 through 50 each on a different card.

RULES: A player shuffles the deck of digit cards and deals three digit cards, face-up, to each player. The rest of the digit cards are placed, face-up, in the center of the table. Next, the deck of whole number cards is shuffled and placed face-up in front of the dealer.

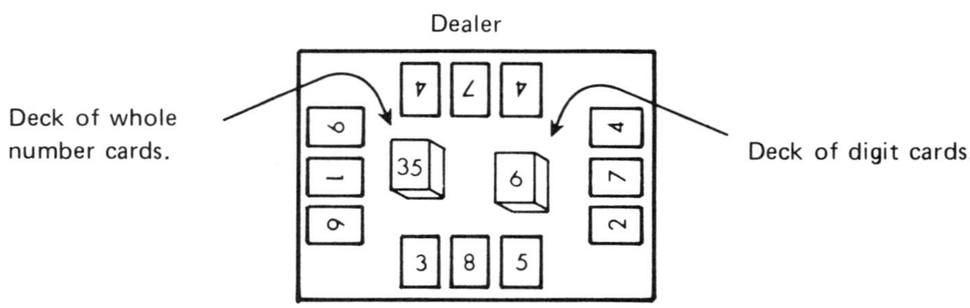

To play the game, the first player to the left of the dealer looks at the top number on the whole number deck and checks the numbers on his three cards for factors of that top number. If he has any, he turns them face-down and replaces them with cards from the digit deck. Play is continued in this manner until every player has checked his cards for factors of the top number. Then the dealer places the top card at the bottom of the deck and play resumes. The game ends when a player turns down his last factor card. When this is done, each player counts his turned-down factor cards. The player with the greatest number wins the game.

As a variation of the above game, at the conclusion of a play, have the player say, "check." If another player thinks that that player overlooked a factor he says, "challenge" and points out such a factor. If the challenger is correct he gets the card. If not, he gives a card to the challenged player.

VARIATION 2: Multiple Turn-Down

MAJOR CONCEPT: Multiples of numbers 1 through 10

NUMBER OF PLAYERS: Two or more

MATERIALS: 1. Four each of the following digit cards:

1	2	3	4	5	6	7	8	9

2. The whole numbers from 1 through 50, each on a different card.

RULES: Multiple Turn-Down is played in a similar way to Factor Turn-Down, but in this game, each player is dealt three cards, face-up, from the whole number deck. The rest of the deck is placed in the center of the table. The deck of digit cards is shuffled and placed face-up in front of the dealer. The object of the game is to turn down multiples of the top number on the digit deck.

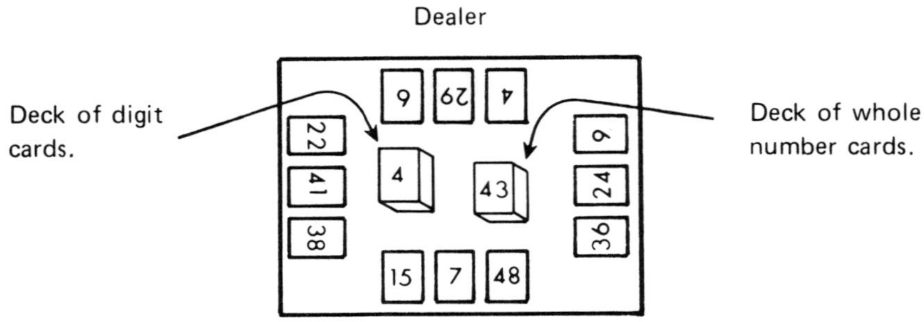

BUILD—A—NUMBER

VARIATION 1: Build-the-Greatest-Whole Number

MAJOR CONCEPT: Whole number place value

NUMBER OF PLAYERS: Two or more

MATERIALS: 1. Paper and pencil for each player.
2. Four each of the following digit cards:

0	1	2	3	4	5	6	7	8	9

RULES: Each player makes a copy of this place value grid:

and places it in front of her on the table. A player shuffles the deck and places it face-up in the center of the table.

To play the game, the first player to the left of the person who shuffled copies the top digit in any one of her four squares. She then turns the top card face-down beside the deck. The next player copies the top digit in any one of her four squares and then turns the top card face-down. Play continues until all players have recorded a digit in each of their four squares. If all the digit cards are used before all squares are filled, the face-down deck is shuffled, turned face-up, and used again. The player who builds the greatest four digit number wins the game.

An obvious variation of the above game is Build-the-Least-Whole Number. A player should be allowed to enter a 0 in her extreme left square. For example, a player could complete her form this way:

0	9	7	3

If so, she would beat any other player who entered a non zero digit in the left-hand square. Slight variations of both games can be made by extending the place value forms as shown below.

VARIATION 2: Build-the-Greatest Decimal

MAJOR CONCEPT: Decimal place value

NUMBER OF PLAYERS: Two or more

MATERIALS: Same as for Build-the-Greatest-Whole Number.

RULES: Build-the-Greatest-Decimal is played in a similar way to Build-the-Greatest-Whole Number but uses this place value form:

$\square\square . \square\square$

A variation would be Build-the-Least-Decimal. Of course, other place value forms can be used for either game. Below are two examples.

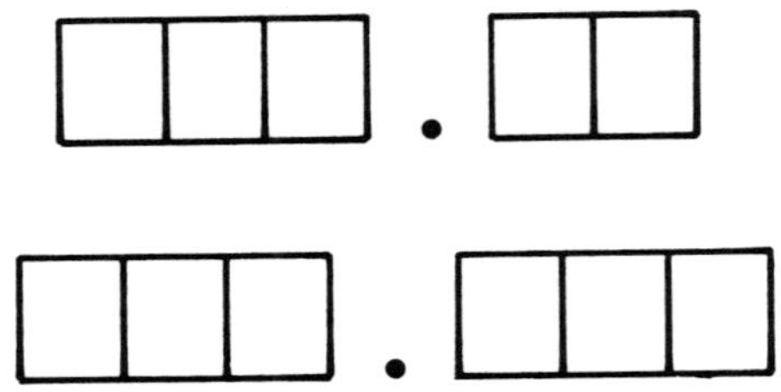

MATCH—A—FACT

VARIATION 1: Match-A-Sum

MAJOR CONCEPT: Basic addition facts

NUMBER OF PLAYERS: Two to four

MATERIALS: 1. Four each of the following digit cards:

0 1 2 3 4 5 6 7 8 9

2. One each of the following sum cards:

0 1 2 3 4 5 6 7 8 9

10 11 12 13 14 15 16 17 18

RULES: The dealer shuffles the digit-deck and deals four cards to each player. Each player puts his cards face-up in front of him. Then the dealer shuffles the sum-deck and places it face-up in the center of the table.

To play the game, the first player to the left of the dealer looks at the top card on the sum-deck. If he has in his own cards two numbers whose sum is the top card number, he turns them face-down and replaces them by drawing two more cards from the digit-deck. He then turns the top card of the sum-deck face-down and play continues. If he does not have two numbers whose sum is the top number, he passes and the next player plays or passes. If all players have to pass, the first player to do so turns the top card face-down and considers the next sum. Play continues until a player has turned down twelve digit cards. The first player to do so is the winner. If all of the sum-deck is used before the game is concluded, it is turned over and play continues.

A slight variation of the above game is to deal more than four digit-cards to each player. Another variation would be to allow a player to turn down two or more addends. For example,

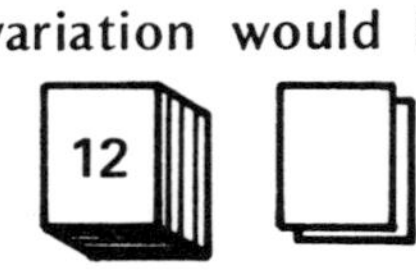

Since 3 + 2 + 7 = 12, all three cards could be turned face-down.

3 2 8 7

VARIATION 2: Match-A-Product

MAJOR CONCEPT: Basic multiplication facts

NUMBER OF PLAYERS: Two to four

MATERIALS: 1. Four each of the following digit cards:

0	1	2	3	4	5	6	7	8	9

2. One each of the following product cards:

0	1	2	3	4	5	6	7	8	9
10	12	14	15	16	18	20	21	24	25
27	30	32	35	36	40	42	45	48	49
54	56	63	64	72	81				

RULES: Match-A-Product is played in a similar way to Match-A-Sum. It will proceed slower since there are fewer basic combinations for a given product than for a given sum. Because of this, it is recommended that each player plays with five digit-cards.

SNAKE

VARIATION 1: Subtraction–Snake

MAJOR CONCEPT: Basic subtraction facts

NUMBER OF PLAYERS: Two or more

MATERIALS: One each of the following cards:

9 – 9 0	8 – 8 1	7 – 7 2	6 – 6 3	5 – 5 4	4 – 4 5	3 – 3 6	2 – 2 7	1 – 1 8	0 – 0 9
10 – 9 0	9 – 8 1	8 – 7 2	7 – 6 3	6 – 5 4	5 – 4 5	4 – 3 6	3 – 2 7	2 – 1 8	1 – 0 9
11 – 9 0	10 – 8 1	9 – 7 2	8 – 6 3	7 – 5 4	6 – 4 5	5 – 3 6	4 – 2 7	3 – 1 8	2 – 0 9
12 – 9 0	11 – 8 1	10 – 7 2	9 – 6 3	8 – 5 4	7 – 4 5	6 – 3 6	5 – 2 7	4 – 1 8	3 – 0 9
13 – 9 0	12 – 8 1	11 – 7 2	10 – 6 3	9 – 5 4	8 – 4 5	7 – 3 6	6 – 2 7	5 – 1 8	4 – 0 9
14 – 9 0	13 – 8 1	12 – 7 2	11 – 6 3	10 – 5 4	9 – 4 5	8 – 3 6	7 – 2 7	6 – 1 8	5 – 0 9
15 – 9 0	14 – 8 1	13 – 7 2	12 – 6 3	11 – 5 4	10 – 4 5	9 – 3 6	8 – 2 7	7 – 1 8	6 – 0 9
16 – 9 0	15 – 8 1	14 – 7 2	13 – 6 3	12 – 5 4	11 – 4 5	10 – 3 6	9 – 2 7	8 – 1 8	7 – 0 9
17 – 9 0	16 – 8 1	15 – 7 2	14 – 6 3	13 – 5 4	12 – 4 5	11 – 3 6	10 – 2 7	9 – 1 8	8 – 0 9
18 – 9 0	17 – 8 1	16 – 7 2	15 – 6 3	14 – 5 4	13 – 4 5	12 – 3 6	11 – 2 7	10 – 1 8	9 – 0 9

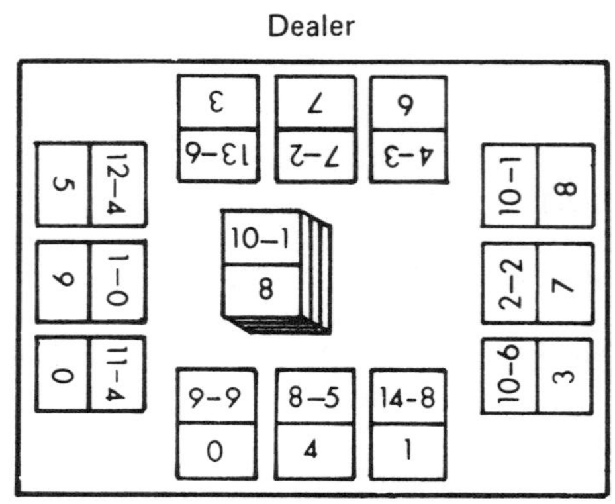

RULES: The dealer shuffles the deck and deals each player three cards face-up. Then she places the rest of the deck, face-up, in front of her. At this point, the situation should look like this:

Starting with the player to the left of the dealer, each player in turn checks to see if any of her cards are doubles. A double is a card showing matching halves:

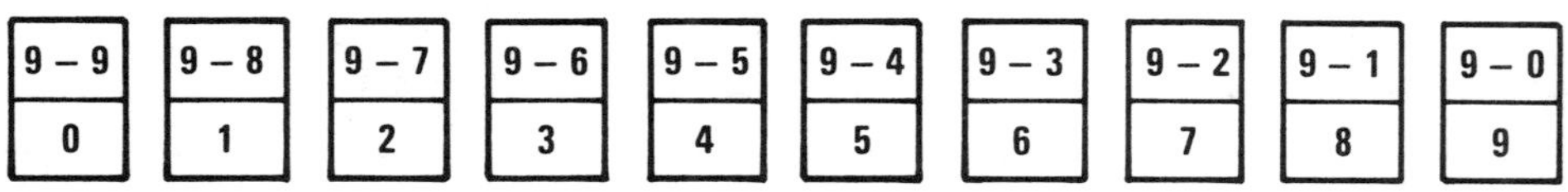

The first player having a double places it face-up in the center of the table. If no player has a double, each player in turn draws the top card from the deck until a double is drawn. Each player puts the non-double cards that she draws with her other cards. After the first double has been played, the next player looks at her cards to see if she has a card that has the number that matches the value of the difference in the subtraction problem in the first double, or a card that has the subtraction problem that matches the difference half of the first double.

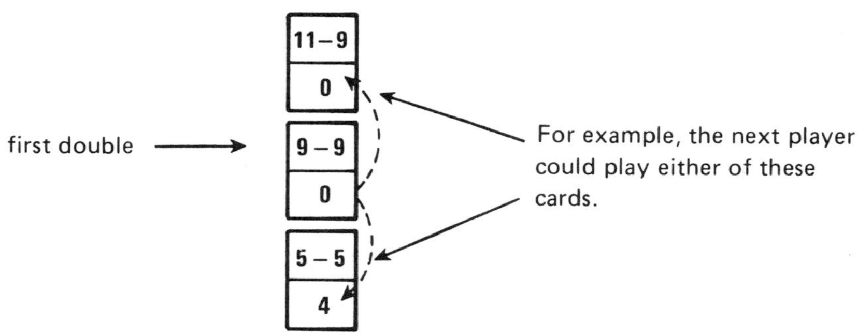

If she cannot play a match, she must draw the top card from the deck and place it face-up in front of her. When any other doubles are played, they are played crosswise and then are open for play on both ends.

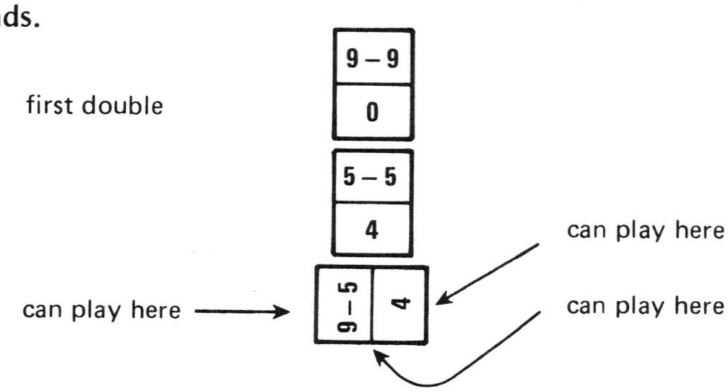

Play continues in this manner. The first player to play all of her cards is the winner.

VARIATION 2: Division-Snake

MAJOR CONCEPT: Basic division facts

NUMBER OF PLAYERS: Two or more

MATERIALS: One each of the following cards:

0÷1	0÷2	0÷3	0÷4	0÷5	0÷6	0÷7	0÷8	0÷9
0	1	2	3	4	5	6	7	8
1÷1	2÷2	3÷3	4÷4	5÷5	6÷6	7÷7	8÷8	9÷9
9	0	1	2	3	4	5	6	7
2÷1	4÷2	6÷3	8÷4	10÷5	12÷6	14÷7	16÷8	18÷9
8	9	0	1	2	3	4	5	6
3÷1	6÷2	9÷3	12÷4	15÷5	18÷6	21÷7	24÷8	27÷9
7	8	9	0	1	2	3	4	5
4÷1	8÷2	12÷3	16÷4	20÷5	24÷6	28÷7	32÷8	36÷9
6	7	8	9	0	1	2	3	4
5÷1	10÷2	15÷3	20÷4	25÷5	30÷6	35÷7	40÷8	45÷9
5	6	7	8	9	0	1	2	3
6÷1	12÷2	18÷3	24÷4	30÷5	36÷6	42÷7	48÷8	54÷9
4	5	6	7	8	9	0	1	2
7÷1	14÷2	21÷3	28÷4	35÷5	42÷6	49÷7	56÷8	63÷9
3	4	5	6	7	8	9	0	1
8÷1	16÷2	24÷3	32÷4	40÷5	48÷6	56÷7	64÷8	72÷9
2	3	4	5	6	7	8	9	0
9÷1	18÷2	27÷3	36÷4	45÷5	54÷6	63÷7	72÷8	81÷9
1	2	3	4	5	6	7	8	9

RULES: Division-Snake is played in a similar way to Subtraction-Snake but uses the division cards.

VARIATION 3: Subtraction and Division Facts

NUMBER OF PLAYERS: Two or more

MATERIALS: Cards shown in Subtraction-Snake and Division-Snake.

RULES: The two decks are shuffled together and the game is played in a similar way to Subtraction-Snake.

ORDER

VARIATION 1: Multiplication Order

MAJOR CONCEPT: Basic multiplication facts

NUMBER OF PLAYERS: Four

MATERIALS: 1. Thirty-three cards of multiplication combinations from 0 through 10 for any three tables, for example, the 3, 4, and 5 tables.

0 x 3 | 1 x 3 | 2 x 3 ------------ 10 x 3

0 x 4 | 1 x 4 | 2 x 4 ------------ 10 x 4

0 x 5 | 1 x 5 | 2 x 5 ------------ 10 x 5

2. Three stands that will hold eight cards in slots. These can be made from wood or styrofoam.

Sample holder:

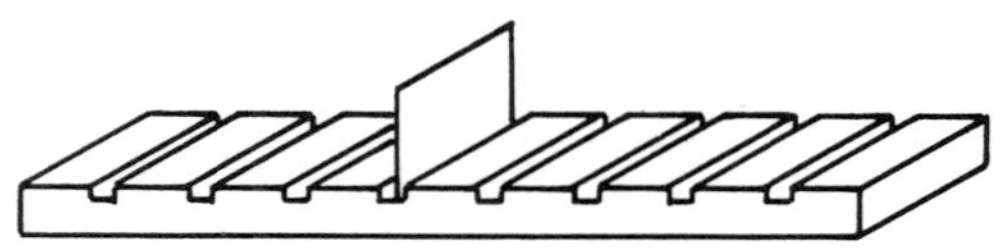

RULES: Each player tries to build a sequence in his stand of eight cards whose products increase from front to back.

Sample card order:

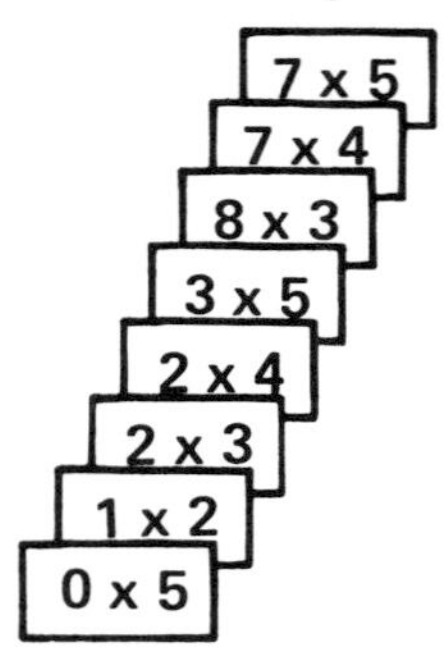

The product on each card must be greater than the one on the card in front of it. The first player to build the sequence is the winner.

To play the game, each player places his stand in front of him so that when the cards are in the slots he can see the faces but the other players cannot. One player shuffles the deck and places it face-down in the center of the table. The first player to the left of the dealer takes the top card of the deck and places it in one of the slots. Once a card is placed in a slot it cannot be moved to another slot. Therefore, the players must plan ahead. Each player, in turn, draws the top card from the deck and places it in a slot. When a player draws a card that he cannot use he discards it face up next to the deck. When there is a discard pile, players may choose either the top card of the deck or the top card of the discard pile.

Although a card cannot be moved from one slot to another, if a player decides that he has made a mistake in placing a card, he may discard that card and replace it with one he has drawn.

The game may be varied by changing the products used. For example, the basic combinations for 5, 6, and 7 can be used instead of those for 3, 4, and 5 as indicated in the sample.

VARIATION 2: Addition Order

MAJOR CONCEPT: Basic addition facts

NUMBER OF PLAYERS: Three

MATERIALS: These 33 cards

0 + 6	1 + 6	------------	10 + 6
0 + 7	1 + 7	------------	10 + 7
0 + 8	1 + 8	------------	10 + 8

RULES: Addition Order is played in a way similar to Multiplication Order.

Variations involving subtraction, division, or combinations of operations can be played.

CARD AND DICE TURN DOWN

VARIATION 1: Addition Fact Turn Down

MAJOR CONCEPT: Basic addition facts

NUMBER OF PLAYERS: Two or more

MATERIALS: 1. Nine digit cards:

1	2	3	4	5	6	7	8	9

2. A pair of dice.

RULES: One player places the nine cards in front of her, face-up, in order. Next, she rolls the dice and adds the two top numbers. Then she turns face-down one or more cards whose sum is the same as that of the dice. For example, if the dice show a total of 6, then the player may turn over the 6 or 1 and 5, or 2 and 4, or 1, 2 and 3, and so on. If the dice show 12, then she could turn 8 and 4, or 6, 4, and 2, or other combinations. Next, she rolls the dice again and turns down more cards. She continues to play until she cannot turn more cards. For example, if these cards remained face-up,

1	2	7

and the player rolled 4 on the dice, she could not turn any cards.

She then computes her score by adding the numbers of the *face-up* cards.

Each player, in turn, plays in the same way. The player with the *lowest* score is the winner.

VARIATION 2: Subtraction-Addition Turn Down

MAJOR CONCEPT: Basic subtraction and addition facts

NUMBER OF PLAYERS: Two or more

MATERIALS: Same as for Addition Fact Turn Down

RULES: Subtraction-Addition Turn Down is played in a similar way to Addition Fact Turn Down, but card numbers can be combined by subtraction as well as by addition. For example, if the dice sum is 7, cards showing 9 and 2 could be turned down because 9 - 2 = 7. Cards showing 5 and 2 could also be turned down since they sum 7.

VARIATION 3: This game is played in a similar way to Addition Fact Turn Down but three dice are used.

BASIC FACTS RUMMY

VARIATION 1: Subtraction Rummy

MAJOR CONCEPT: Basic subtraction facts

NUMBER OF PLAYERS: Two to four

MATERIALS: One each of the following cards:

9 – 9	8 – 8	7 – 7	6 – 6	5 – 5	4 – 4	3 – 3	2 – 2	1 – 1	0 – 0
10 – 9	9 – 8	8 – 7	7 – 6	6 – 5	5 – 4	4 – 3	3 – 2	2 – 1	1 – 0
11 – 9	10 – 8	9 – 7	8 – 6	7 – 5	6 – 4	5 – 3	4 – 2	3 – 1	2 – 0
12 – 9	11 – 8	10 – 7	9 – 6	8 – 5	7 – 4	6 – 3	5 – 2	4 – 1	3 – 0
13 – 9	12 – 8	11 – 7	10 – 6	9 – 5	8 – 4	7 – 3	6 – 2	5 – 1	4 – 0
14 – 9	13 – 8	12 – 7	11 – 6	10 – 5	9 – 4	8 – 3	7 – 2	6 – 1	5 – 0
15 – 9	14 – 8	13 – 7	12 – 6	11 – 5	10 – 4	9 – 3	8 – 2	7 – 1	6 – 0
16 – 9	15 – 8	14 – 7	13 – 6	12 – 5	11 – 4	10 – 3	9 – 2	8 – 1	7 – 0
17 – 9	16 – 8	15 – 7	14 – 6	13 – 5	12 – 4	11 – 3	10 – 2	9 – 1	8 – 0
18 – 9	17 – 8	16 – 7	15 – 6	14 – 5	13 – 4	12 – 3	11 – 2	10 – 1	9 – 0

RULES: The dealer shuffles the deck and deals seven cards to each player. The next card is placed face-up in the center of the table to start the discard pile and the rest of the deck is placed face-down beside it. Each player looks at his own cards and tries to build books of three or four matching cards. Matching cards are cards with the same difference.

Two sample books:

12 – 9	6 – 3	8 – 5

10 – 3	15 – 8	12 – 5	8 – 1

The play moves in a clockwise direction starting with the player on the dealer's left. When it is his turn, a player draws one card, either the top face-down card of the deck or the top face-up card of the discard pile. Then, if he has any books, he may lay them face-up in front of him for everyone to see. If he has one or more cards that match books others have played, he may also play them face-up in front of him. For example, if a player has the (5–1)-card in his hand and another player has played a book for the difference 4, the player may lay the (5–1)–card by itself in front of him pointing out that it fits in someone else's book. Finally, the player must discard one card face–up on the top of the discard pile.

If all the cards in the deck are used before a player goes out, the discard pile, except for the top card, can be shuffled and used as the deck.

Play ends when a player runs out of cards by discarding his last card. At this time players' scores must be recorded. Each player scores one point for every card he has laid down in front of him and loses one point for every card he still holds in his hand. Notice that the player who goes out scores seven points and the other players score fewer.

Next, all of the cards are shuffled and dealt, and play starts again. The game continues until a player scores some predetermined number of points, for example, 50.

Note that a player is not required to lay down a book if he does not wish to. There are sometimes advantages to holding books for several rounds and going out all at once.

VARIATION 2: Division Rummy

MAJOR CONCEPT: Basic division facts

NUMBER OF PLAYERS: Two to four

MATERIALS: One each of the following cards:

0÷1	0÷2	0÷3	0÷4	0÷5	0÷6	0÷7	0÷8	0÷9
1÷1	2÷2	3÷3	4÷4	5÷5	6÷6	7÷7	8÷8	9÷9
2÷1	4÷2	6÷3	8÷4	10÷5	12÷6	14÷7	16÷8	18÷9
3÷1	6÷2	9÷3	12÷4	15÷5	18÷6	21÷7	24÷8	27÷9
4÷1	8÷2	12÷3	16÷4	20÷5	24÷6	28÷7	32÷8	36÷9
5÷1	10÷2	15÷3	20÷4	25÷5	30÷6	35÷7	40÷8	45÷9
6÷1	12÷2	18÷3	24÷4	30÷5	36÷6	42÷7	48÷8	54÷9
7÷1	14÷2	21÷3	28÷4	35÷5	42÷6	49÷7	56÷8	63÷9
8÷1	16÷2	24÷3	32÷4	40÷5	48÷6	56÷7	64÷8	72÷9
9÷1	18÷2	27÷3	36÷4	45÷5	54÷6	63÷7	72÷8	81÷9

RULES: Division Rummy is played in a similar way to Subtraction Rummy, but uses division cards.

NUMBER PAIRS

MAJOR CONCEPT: Basic facts in all operations

NUMBER OF PLAYERS: Two to four

MATERIALS: 45 cards in the pattern started below:

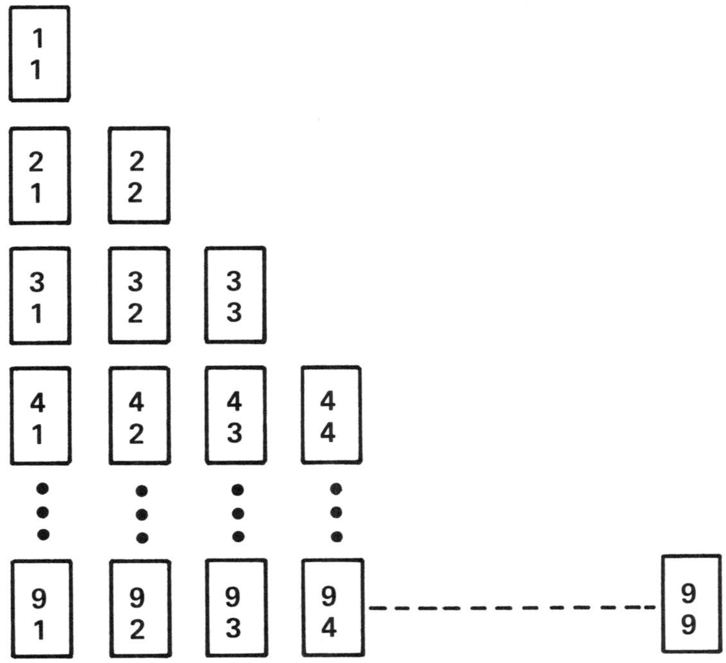

RULES: Several numbers are associated with each card. For example, with [9 / 3] these four numbers are associated:

12 because 9 + 3 = 12

6 because 9 − 3 = 6

27 because 9 x 3 = 27

3 because 9 ÷ 3 = 3

Notice the order in which the two numbers from the card are used — top number first and bottom number second. For a second example, consider the numbers associated with: [2 / 2]

4 because 2 + 2 = 4
and 2 x 2 = 4

0 because 2 − 2 = 0

1 because 2 ÷ 2 = 1

In this case, there are only three numbers for the card. In many cases, the quotient of the numbers on the card is not a whole number, and in the simple variation of this game is not used.

To play the game, the deck is shuffled and five cards are dealt to each player. One card is turned face-up in the center of the table and the rest of the deck is placed face-down next to it. The play starts with the player to the left of the dealer and moves to the left. The first player must find a card in her hand that matches the face-up card and place it face-up on top of that card. To match, two cards must agree in one of their associated numbers. For example, for the face-up card $\boxed{\begin{matrix}8\\2\end{matrix}}$, the four associated numbers are 10, 6, 16, and 4. The first player must play, from her hand, a card that has one of these numbers associated with it. Here are some of the cards she could play.

$\boxed{\begin{matrix}7\\3\end{matrix}}$	because 7 + 3 = 10
$\boxed{\begin{matrix}3\\2\end{matrix}}$	because 3 x 2 = 6
$\boxed{\begin{matrix}4\\4\end{matrix}}$	because 4 x 4 = 16
$\boxed{\begin{matrix}9\\5\end{matrix}}$	because 9 – 5 = 4
$\boxed{\begin{matrix}4\\1\end{matrix}}$	because 4 x 1 = 4

There are, of course, many other cards that could also be played. The player must explain how her card matches the face-up card. If the player does not have a card in her hand to play, she must draw cards until she gets one. After the first player has played, her card is the top face-up card and is the one the next player must match. Play continues in this manner until a player runs out of cards. That player is the winner.

If the deck is used up before there is a winner, the discard pile, except for the top card, is shuffled, placed face-down and used as before.

For children who have worked with fractions, a variation of this game is to use the fractional numbers as well as the whole numbers. For example, $\boxed{\begin{matrix}3\\2\end{matrix}}$ and $\boxed{\begin{matrix}9\\6\end{matrix}}$ match because in both cases the quotient is $\frac{3}{2}$.

LINE-UP

MAJOR CONCEPT: Basic addition facts

NUMBER OF PLAYERS: Two to four

MATERIALS: One hundred cards, each showing one of the basic addition combinations, using numerals 0 through 9.

[0 + 0] [0 + 1] [0 + 2] - - - - - - - - [0 + 9]

[1 + 0] [1 + 1] - - - - - - - - - - [1 + 9]

⋮ ⋮ ⋮

[9 + 0] [9 + 1] - - - - - - - - - - [9 + 9]

RULES: The deck is shuffled and five cards are dealt, face-down, to each player. The next card is turned face-up in the center of the table. The rest of the deck is stacked face-down on the table where all players can reach it. At this stage, a two-player game situation may look like this:

[3 + 5]

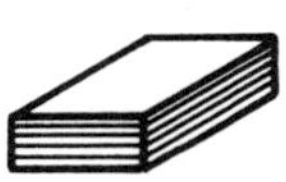

[5 + 6] [8 + 3] [7 + 1] [9 + 6] [3 + 3]

[1 + 1] [8 + 9] [3 + 4] [7 + 7] [9 + 9]

To play the game, players try to build an ordered row of cards, working in both directions, from the first face-up card.

← [6] [7] [3 + 5] [9] [10] [11] →

They may also build ordered columns, building up and down, from the first row of cards.

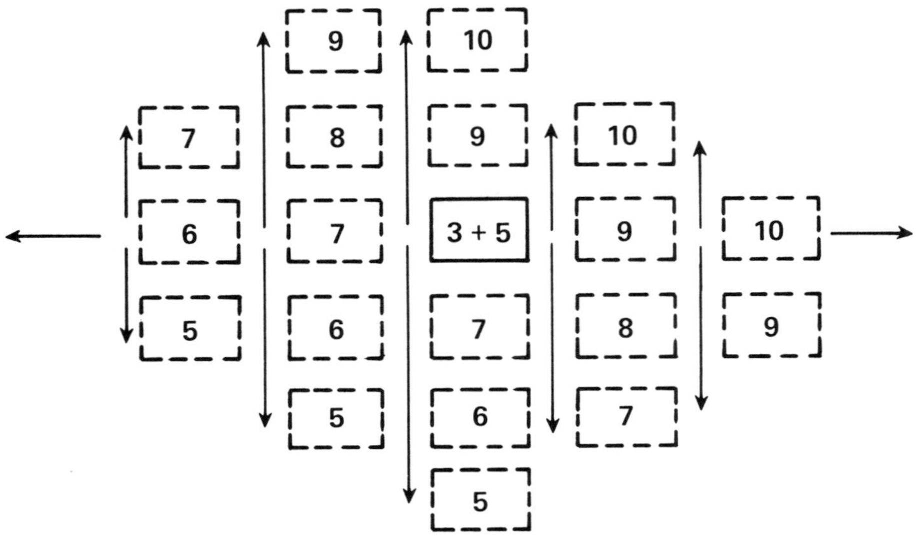

Since the first face-up card is equal to eight, the only cards that the first player, the player on the dealer's left, can play must have either 7 or 9 as the sum. In this example, the first player has a 7-card and can play it to the left of the 8-card.

[3 + 4] [3 + 5]

Now there are more opportunities for the next player.

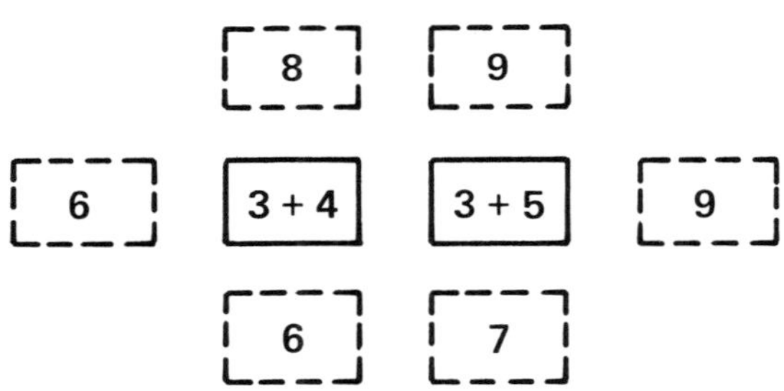

He can play either the [7 + 1] or the [3 + 3] from his hand. Suppose that he plays the [3 + 3].

[3 + 3] [3 + 4] [3 + 5]

The play now returns to the other player. In order to play, he needs a 5-, 6-, 7-, 8-, or 9-card. He has none of these, so he must draw cards, one at a time, from the deck until he gets a card that he can play. The play continues to move from player to player in a clockwise direction. In every case, a player plays a card if he can, or draws from the deck until he gets a card that he can play. The first player to run out of cards is the winner.

Note that cards can be played right or left of other cards only in the row of the first card. All other plays must be above or below other cards. The dashed outlines show places where cards may be played in this example.

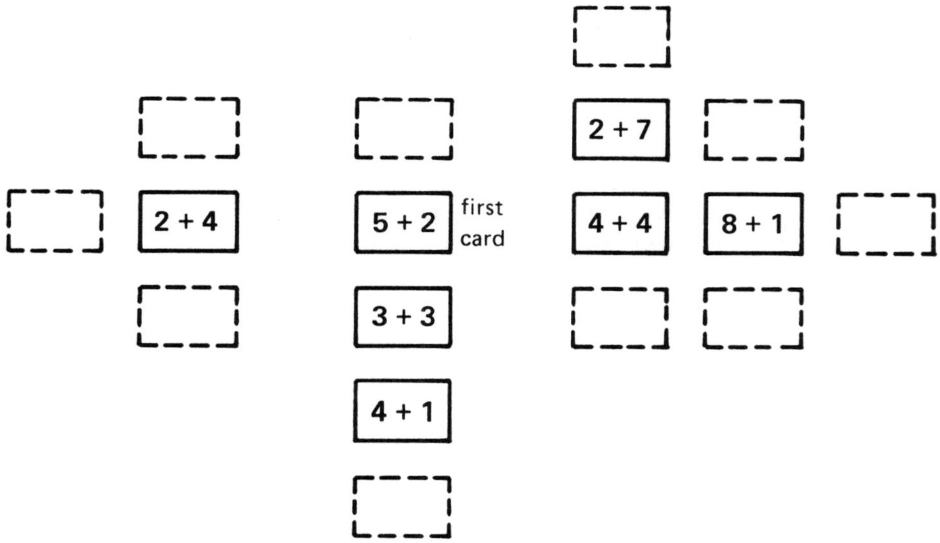
2 + 4
5 + 2
first card
3 + 3
4 + 1
2 + 7
4 + 4
8 + 1

BASIC FACT TRADING

MAJOR CONCEPT: Basic Facts

NUMBER OF PLAYERS: Four to six

MATERIALS: One set of eight basic-fact exercise cards for each player. All of the exercises of a set have the same answer.

Sample set for the number seven:

3 + 4	2 + 5	9 − 2	35 ÷ 5
16 − 9	6 + 1	63 ÷ 9	7 x 1

Here is one set for the number nine:

3 x 3	3 + 6	7 + 2	18 − 9
16 − 7	54 ÷ 6	10 − 1	36 ÷ 4

Other sets of eight cards can be made for the numbers 1, 2, 3, 4, 5, 6, 8, and 10.

If there are four players, there will be four of these sets, making a deck of 32 cards. For six players there will be six sets making a deck of 48 cards.

RULES: One player shuffles the cards and deals them, one at a time, face-down, to the players. Each player will have eight cards which she sorts into sets according to the answer of the exercises. For example, a player holding these cards would sort them as shown.

7 set	10 set	9 set	4 set
3 + 4, 6 + 1, 63 ÷ 9, 9 − 2	2 x 5, 20 ÷ 2	18 − 9	2 x 2

The object of the game is to get all eight cards of the same set by trading cards, sight unseen, with the other players. The first player to complete a set is the winner.

To trade, each player selects from her hand some cards that she wishes to trade, holds them face-down in front of her, and calls out the number of cards until she finds someone who will trade an equal number of cards with her. For example, if a player wishes to trade three cards, she will hold the three cards in front of her face-down and call out "Three! Three!" until she finds someone who will trade three cards with her. After making a trade, the player looks at her new cards, keeps the ones she wants, and then tries to arrange another trade. Players continue to trade in this way until someone collects all eight cards in one set. She shows her cards for the other players to check. If she has made no error, she is the winner.

A player is never forced to trade with another player. Also, a player may change her mind about the number of cards she wishes to exchange before she has made the trade.

RIGHT ON THE NOSE

VARIATION I: Addition-on-the-Nose

MAJOR CONCEPT: Addition practice

NUMBER OF PLAYERS: Two or three

MATERIALS: Four each of the following digit cards:

0 1 2 3 4 5 6 7 8 9

RULES: One player shuffles and deals three cards to each player and places the deck face-down in the center of the table. The players look at their cards but do not show them to other players. The play starts with the player to the left of the dealer and rotates clockwise. The first player puts one of his cards face-up in the middle of the table and then takes the top card of the deck. The next player places one of his cards on top of that card and announces the sum of the two numbers. Then, he takes the top card from the deck. The next player places one of his cards on top of the preceding two, and adds his number to the earlier sum. He also replaces the card by taking the top card of the deck. For example:

Play continues until one player makes the sum exactly 21. That player is the winner.

No player is allowed to play a number that makes the sum greater than 21. If a player does not have a card that he can play, he passes and takes the top card from the deck. If a player announces the wrong sum, he takes back his card and loses his chance to play the round.

One way to vary the game is to change the winning number. For example, aim for 35 instead of 21.

VARIATION 2: Addition and Subtraction On-the-Nose

MAJOR CONCEPT: Addition and subtraction practice

NUMBER OF PLAYERS: Two or three

MATERIALS: Same as for Addition-on-the-Nose

RULES: This game is played in a similar way to Addition-on-the-Nose but numbers can be played to sum greater than 21. Whenever the sum is greater than 21 the next numbers are subtracted instead of added until a player lands on 21. Once again, the first player to land on 21 is the winner. The number aimed for can be varied.

Another variation is to allow multiplication and division, as well as addition and subtraction, to arrive at the goal number.

NUMBER RUMMY

MAJOR CONCEPT: Computation accuracy

NUMBER OF PLAYERS: Two to five

MATERIALS: Eight each of the following digit cards:

[0] [1] [2] [3] [4] [5] [6] [7] [8] [9]

RULES: One player shuffles the deck and deals seven cards, face-down, to each player. Then she places the remainder of the deck face-down in the center of the table and, finally, turns the top card of the deck face-up next to the deck. This card starts the discard pile. Each player builds books of two or more cards whose numbers combine in some way to make 10. The numbers may be combined using any operation the player knows.

Sample books:

[3] [4] [2]
$(3 \times 4) - 2 = 10$

[2] [5]
$2 \times 5 = 10$

[6] [4]
$6 + 4 = 10$

[2] [3] [3] [1]
$(2 \times 3) + 3 + 1 = 10$

[6] [5] [3]
$(6 \times 5) \div 3 = 10$

[3] [2] [1]
$3^2 + 1 = 10$

Starting with the player to the left of the dealer, players may draw either the top card of the deck or the top card of the discard pile, and discard one card, face-up, on the discard pile. After each player draws a card, and before she discards, she may put down in front of her any of her books, explaining them as she does so. Play continues in this manner until a player runs out of cards by laying down a book and discarding her last card. If all of the cards in the deck are used before someone goes out, the discard pile, except for the top card, is shuffled, placed face-down and used again. Each player then gets one point for each card she has in her books, and loses one point for each card left in her hand. The player who goes out gets seven points while the other players win fewer. The cards are dealt again and play continues. The first player to get 50 or more points is the winner.

The game can be varied by changing the book number. For example, players could build 30 instead of 10.

EQUATIONS RUMMY

VARIATION 1: One-Equation Rummy

MAJOR CONCEPT: Practice in all operations

NUMBER OF PLAYERS: Two to four

MATERIALS: Four each of the following digit cards:

[0] [1] [2] [3] [4] [5] [6] [7] [8] [9]

RULES: One player shuffles the deck and deals four cards to each player. The next card is turned face-up in the middle of the table to begin a discard pile next to the rest of the deck turned face-down. Each player looks at her cards for numbers to be used to form an equation. For example, these numbers could form an equation

[2] [1] [4] [9]

because $(2 \times 4) + 1 = 9$.

These numbers could also form an equation

[3] [5] [6] [9]

because $3 \times 5 = 6 + 9$.

If the first player, the person to the left of the dealer, has four cards that form an equation, she explains her equation to the other players and is the winner of the round. If she does not have an equation, she draws either the top card of the deck or the top card of the discard pile and discards one card. If the next player has an equation, she explains it and is the winner. If not, she draws. Play continues in this way until a player has an equation. The winner of a round gets one point. Then the cards are shuffled and dealt again, this time by the player to the left of the first dealer. Play continues until one player gets a total of 10 points. She is the winner of the game.

Once a player has decided that she does not have an equation and draws a card, she cannot go back and correct an error. For example, if a player's cards form an equation but the player does not recognize it until after she draws a card, she cannot show the equation and win the round. She must wait until it is her turn again.

If the deck is depleted before there is a winner, the discard pile, except for the top card, is shuffled and used as the deck.

One variation of this game is to deal five cards instead of four.

VARIATION 2: Many-Equations Rummy

NUMBER OF PLAYERS: Two to four

MATERIALS: Same as for One-Equation Rummy.

RULES: In this game, seven cards are dealt to each player. Players separate the numbers into equations, but, in this game, they may build more than one equation.

For example, this is a winning hand:

2	5	2	3	4	6	6

$$\frac{(2 \times 5) + 2}{3} = 4 \qquad 6 = 6$$

This is also a winning hand:

3	2	6	3	6	2	9

$$3 \times 2 = 6 \qquad 3 \times 6 = 2 \times 9$$

The method of keeping score can be the same as that of One-Equation Rummy. Another way of scoring, however, is for all players to display as many equations as they can when the first player goes out. Then each player gets one point for each card that she has displayed, and loses one point for each card still in her hand. In this case, a player wins when she has 50 or more points.

ARITHMETIC FISHIN'

MAJOR CONCEPT: Arithmetic practice

NUMBER OF PLAYERS: Two to six

MATERIALS: Twelve sets of four cards. In each set the cards have different combinations for the same number.

Sample set for 20:	$40 \div 2$	$24 - 4$	4×5	$15 + 5$
Sample set for 36:	4×9	6×6	$23 + 13$	$43 - 7$

RULES: One player shuffles the cards, deals five cards to each player, and places the rest of the deck face-down in the center of the table. Each player then discards pairs of matching cards, that is, pairs of cards from the same set. Each discarded pair is shown to the other players so they can check for errors. After all matching pairs have been discarded, play begins. Play starts with the player to the left of the dealer and moves to the left. When it is his turn, a player asks the player on his right for a card for a specific number. For example, he may say, "Give me a 20," or "Give me a 36." If the player who is asked has such a card, he must give it to the player who asked for it. If the asked player does not have such a card, then the player who asked must take a card from the deck. In either case, if pairs are formed, they are shown and discarded. The first player to run out of cards is the winner. Two players may run out of cards on the same play and tie as winners.

TARGET NUMBER

MAJOR CONCEPT: Basic combination

NUMBER OF PLAYERS: Two or more

MATERIALS: 1. Paper and pencil for each player.

2. Four each of the following digit cards:

[0] [1] [2] [3] [4] [5] [6] [7] [8] [9]

RULES: Each player draws a copy of the following target number form.

$$(\square + \square) + (\square + \square) \longrightarrow 20$$

(This form could be prepared beforehand with a duplicating master.) The digit-deck is shuffled and placed, face-up, in the center of the table.

To play the game, the player to the left of the player who shuffled, copies the top-digit in any one of her four squares. Then the top-digit card is turned face-down beside the digit-deck. Play continues in this manner until all players have filled in their four squares. Each player adds her four numbers. The player with the sum nearest the target number, 20, wins the game.

Sample play:

(16) $(\boxed{3} + \boxed{4}) + (\boxed{6} + \boxed{3}) \longrightarrow 20$

(26) $(\boxed{9} + \boxed{4}) + (\boxed{5} + \boxed{8}) \longrightarrow 20$

(17) $(\boxed{2} + \boxed{0}) + (\boxed{8} + \boxed{7}) \longrightarrow 20$

(18) $(\boxed{5} + \boxed{5}) + (\boxed{6} + \boxed{2}) \longrightarrow 20$ ← This player would win the game.

An unlimited number of variations can be obtained by changing the target number form. For example, a target number form such as this,

$$(\square + \square) + (\square - \square) \longrightarrow 6$$

could be used to practice basic combinations in both addition and subtraction. When subtraction is involved, a new rule will have to be introduced: if a player fills her squares so that the subtraction is impossible, she is disqualified from that game. For example, a player who filled her squares like this, would be disqualified.

$$(\boxed{3} + \boxed{4}) + (\boxed{6} - \boxed{8}) \longrightarrow 6$$

The following target number forms can also be used to practice basic combinations.

$$(\square - \square) + (\square + \square) \longrightarrow 10$$

$$(\square - \square) + (\square \times \square) \longrightarrow 30$$

$$(\square \times \square) - (\square + \square) \longrightarrow 15$$

$$(\square \times \square) - (\square - \square) \longrightarrow 20$$

$$(\square + \square) \times (\square - \square) \longrightarrow 30$$

THIRTY-ONE

VARIATION 1: Addition Thirty-one

MAJOR CONCEPT: Addition practice

NUMBER OF PLAYERS: Two to four

MATERIALS: Four each of these digit cards:

0	1	2	3	4	5	6	7	8	9

RULES: One player shuffles the cards, deals five cards face-down to each player, turns the next card face-up in the center of the table to start the discard pile, and places the rest of the deck face-down next to it. The players try to collect five cards whose numbers total 31. The first player to do so wins the round. Play begins with the player on the dealer's left. If his cards total 31, he is the winner. If not, he may draw the top card of the deck or the top card of the discard pile. Then he discards one card face-up on the discard pile. Play continues in this way until a player has five cards totaling 31. The winner scores one point. The next round is dealt by the player to the left of the first dealer. The winner of the game is the first player to get ten points.

For variety, a number different from 31 could be used as the goal.

VARIATION 2: Addition-Subtraction Thirty-one

MAJOR CONCEPT: Addition and subtraction practice

NUMBER OF PLAYERS: Two to four

MATERIALS: Same as Addition Thirty-one.

RULES: This game is played in a similar way to Addition Thirty-one but the numbers on the five cards can be subtracted as well as added. For example, this is a winning hand,

9	8	9	7	2

because $9 + 8 + 9 + 7 - 2 = 31$.

BUILD-AN-ANSWER (WHOLE NUMBER)

VARIATION 1: Build-The-Greatest-Sum

MAJOR CONCEPT: Addition algorithm

NUMBER OF PLAYERS: Two or more

MATERIALS: 1. Paper and pencil for each player.

2. Four each of the following digit cards:

[0] [1] [2] [3] [4] [5] [6] [7] [8] [9]

RULES: Each player makes a copy of this addition form

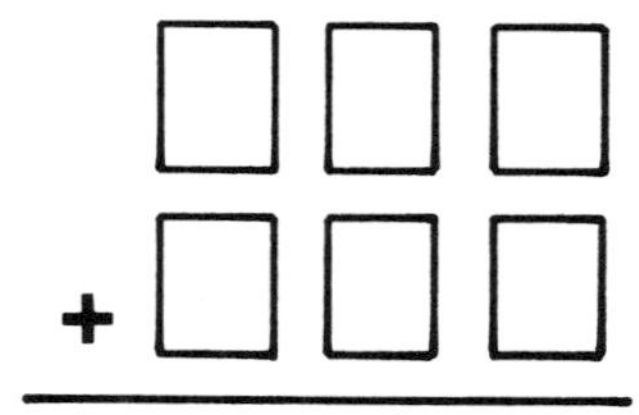

and places it in front of him on the table. (Since each player will need to copy the addition form before the play of each game, it would expedite play to prepare several copies of the form using a duplicating master.) One player shuffles the deck and places it face-up in the center of the table.

To play the game, the first person to the left of the player who shuffled, copies the top digit in any of her six squares not allowing the other players to see which square was filled in. She then turns the top card face-down alongside the deck.

The next player copies the top digit in one of her squares and then turns the top card face-down. Play continues in this manner until all players have filled in all of their squares. If all the digit cards are used before all squares are filled in, the face-down deck should be turned over and play continued. After the game ends, each player computes her sum. The player having the greatest sum wins the game. The other players should check the winner's addition.

A variation of the game is Build-The-Least-Sum. In this game, the player who builds the least sum wins. The addition form can also be changed. Here are some other addition forms that can be used to play Build-The-Greatest-Sum or Build-The-Least-Sum.

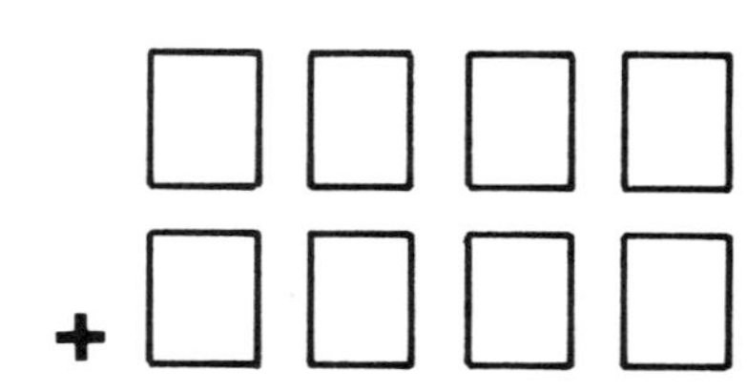

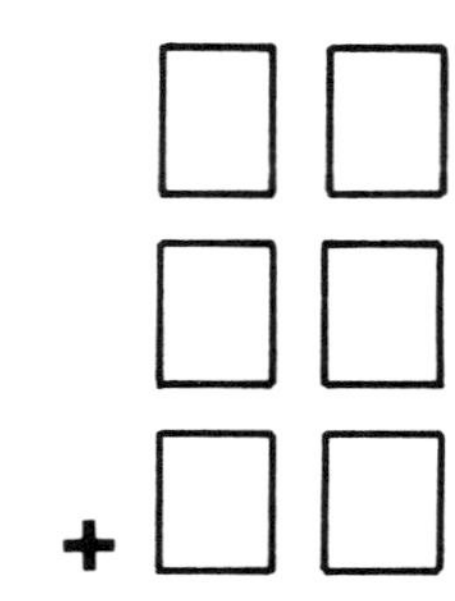

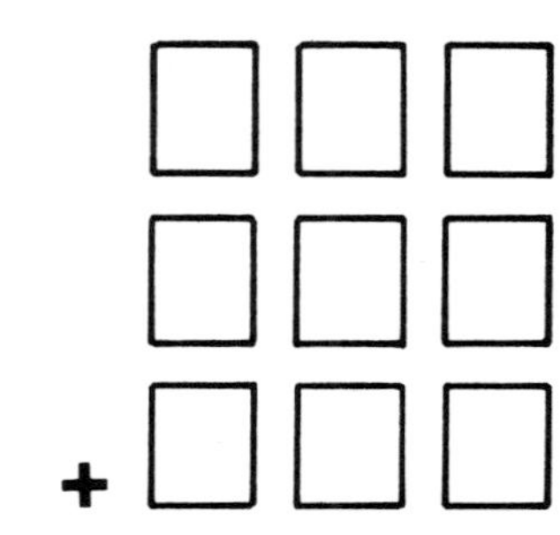

VARIATION 2: Build-The-Greatest-Difference

MAJOR CONCEPT: Subtraction algorithm

NUMBER OF PLAYERS: Two or more

MATERIALS: Same as for Build-The-Greatest-Sum

RULES: Build-The-Greatest-Difference is played in a similar way to Build-The-Greatest-Sum, using the following subtraction form:

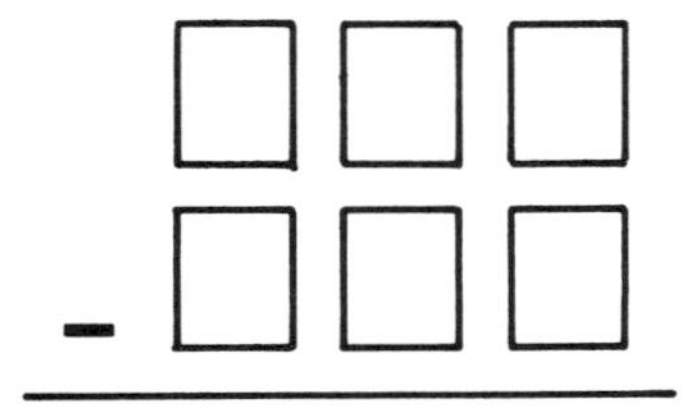

However, because the game uses subtraction rather than addition, it has one additional rule: if a player fills her squares in such a way that the subtraction is impossible, she is disqualified from that game. For example, a player who filled her subtraction form like this:

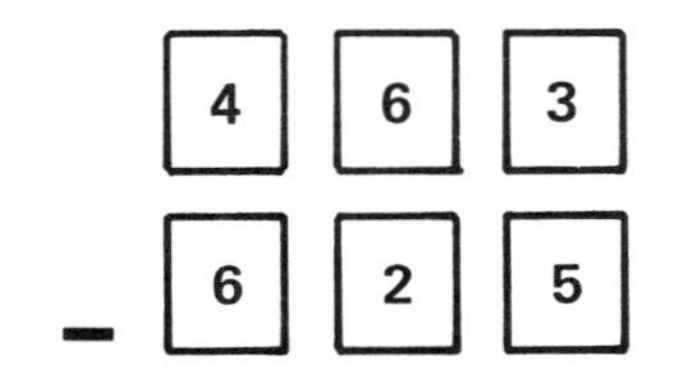

would be disqualified.

One variation of this game is Build-The-Least-Difference. Another variation is to change the subtraction form. For example, here is another subtraction form that can be used to play Build-The-Greatest-Difference or Build-The-Least-Difference.

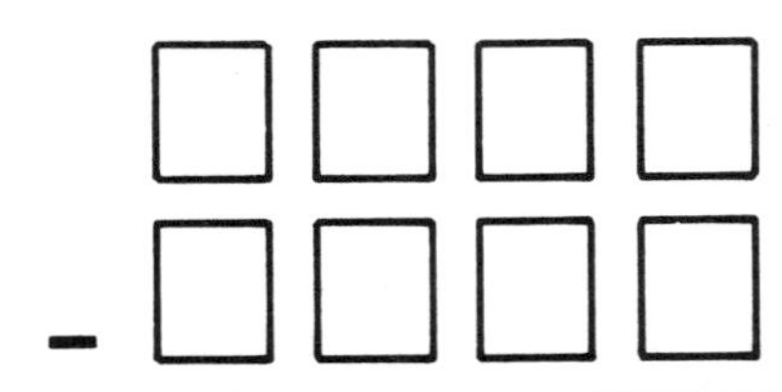

VARIATION 3: Build-The-Greatest-Product

MAJOR CONCEPT: Multiplication algorithm

NUMBER OF PLAYERS: Two or more

MATERIALS: Same as for Build-The-Greatest-Sum

RULES: Build-The-Greatest-Product is played in a similar way to Build-The-Greatest-Sum but uses multiplication. It can be played with this multiplication form:

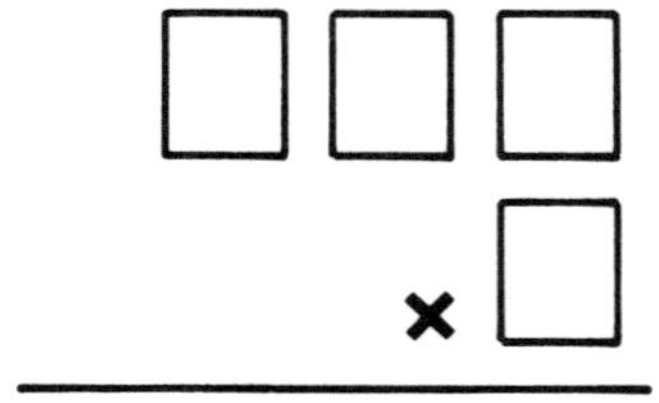

Variations of the game include Build-The-Least-Product and changing the multiplication form. Below are some other forms that can be used to play Build-The-Greatest-Product or Build-The-Least-Product.

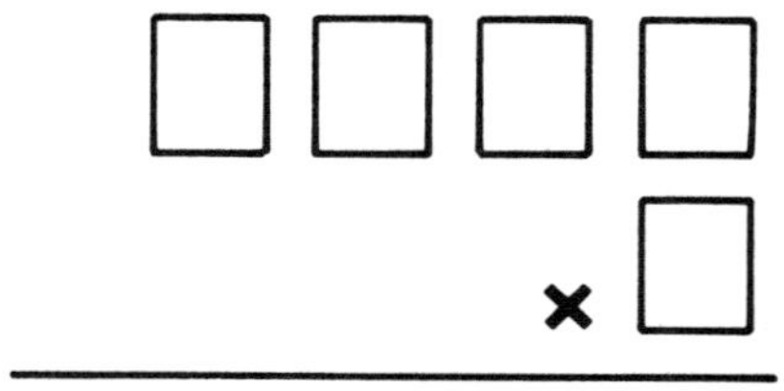 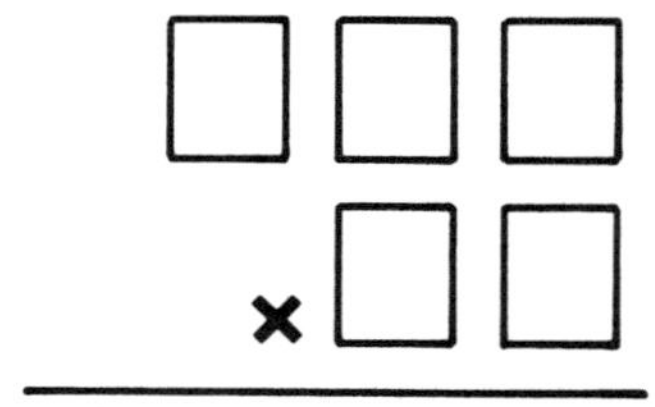

VARIATION 4: Build-The-Greatest-Quotient

MAJOR CONCEPT: Division algorithm

NUMBER OF PLAYERS: Two or more

MATERIALS: Same as for Build-The-Greatest-Sum

RULES: Build-The-Greatest-Quotient is played in a similar way to Build-The-Greatest-Sum, using this division form:

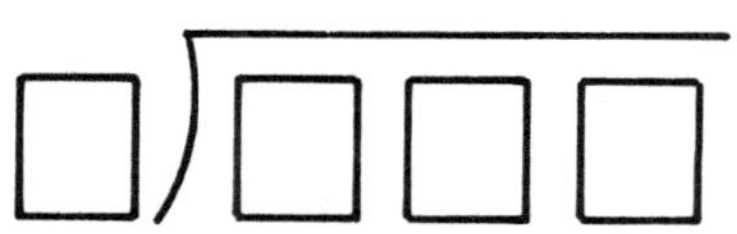

However, because the game uses division, it has one additional rule: if a player ends up with zero as the divisor she is disqualified from that game. For example, a player who filled in her squares like this:

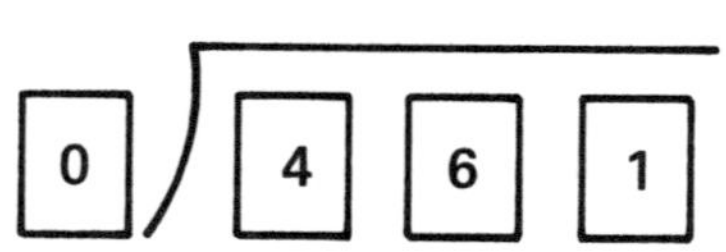

would be disqualified, since division by 0 is undefined.

Variations can be obtained by playing Build-The-Least-Quotient and by changing the division form. For example, either of these forms

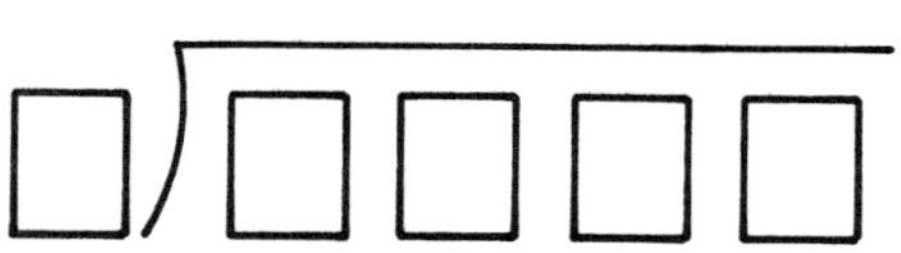 

can be used to play Build-The-Greatest-Quotient or Build-The-Least-Quotient.

BUILD-A-PROBLEM

VARIATION 1: Build-An-Addition-Problem

MAJOR CONCEPT: Addition algorithm

NUMBER OF PLAYERS: Two or more

MATERIALS: 1. Paper and pencil for each player.

2. Four each of the following digit cards:

0 1 2 3 4 5 6 7 8 9

RULES: Each player makes a copy of this addition form:

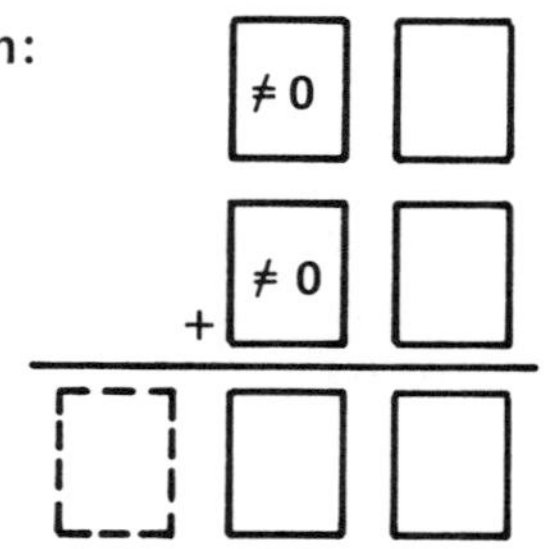

and places it in front of him on the table. (Since each player will need to copy the addition form before the play of each game, it would expedite play to prepare several copies of the form using a duplicating master.) A player shuffles the deck and places it face-up in the center of the table.

The object of the game is to use the top digit of the deck to build a completed addition problem. The solid squares must all be filled and the squares containing a $\neq 0$ cannot be filled with a zero. The dotted square may or may not be filled. This will depend on the digits entered in the solid squares.

To play the game, the player to the left of the player who shuffled, enters the top digit in one of his squares. He then turns the top card face-down and places it beside the deck. The next player enters the new top digit in one of his squares and then turns the card face-down. Play continues in this manner. If a player cannot use the top digit he must leave the top card face-up and pass. The next player then uses the number or passes. If everyone passes, the top card is turned face-down and the first player who passed considers the next digit. The first player to build a completed addition problem wins the game. If all the digit cards are used before a player wins, the face-down deck should be turned over and play continued. The other players should check the winner's problem.

A slight variation of the above game can be obtained by changing the addition form. Some other addition forms that can be used to play Build-An-Addition-Problem are on the next page.

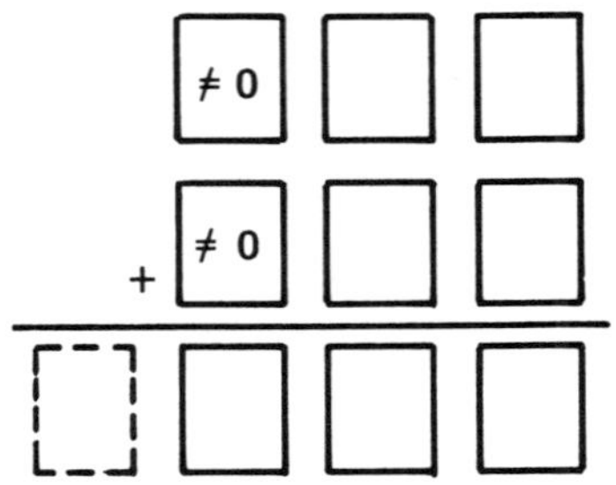

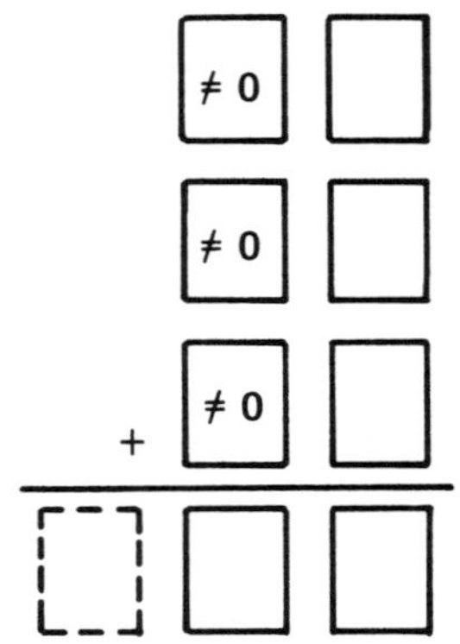

VARIATION 2: Build-A-Subtraction-Problem

MAJOR CONCEPT: Subtraction algorithm

NUMBER OF PLAYERS: Two or more

MATERIALS: Same as for Build-An-Addition-Problem

RULES: Build-A-Subtraction-Problem is played in a similar way to Build-An-Addition-Problem, but uses subtraction. It can be played with this subtraction form:

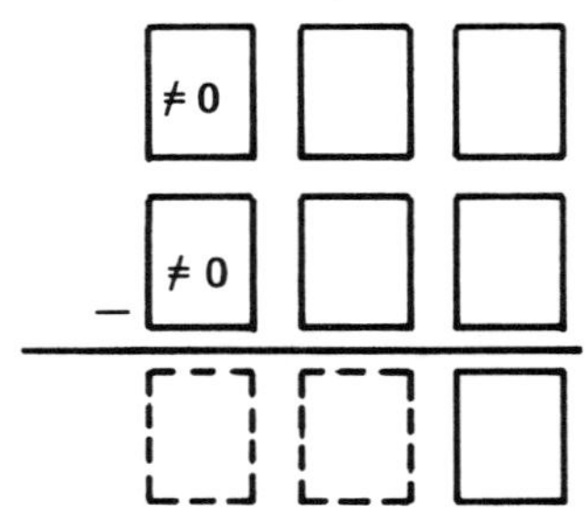

Build-A-Subtraction-Problem can be varied by using a different subtraction form, such as:

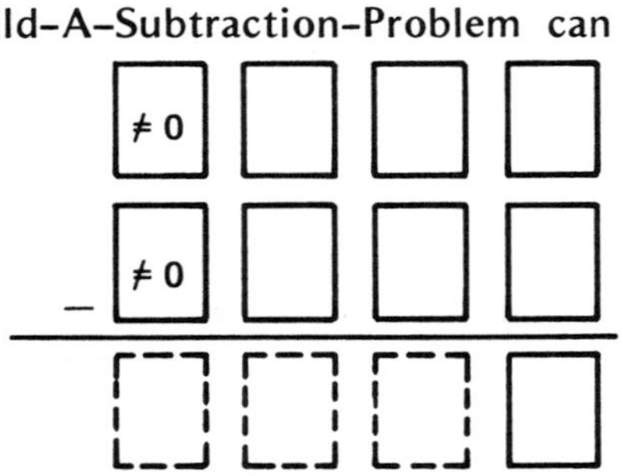

VARIATION 3: Build-A-Multiplication-Problem

MAJOR CONCEPT: Multiplication algorithm

NUMBER OF PLAYERS: Two or more

MATERIALS: Same as for Build-An-Addition-Problem

RULES: Build-A-Multiplication-Problem is played in a similar way to Build-An-Addition-Problem, but it uses multiplication. Either of the following multiplication forms can be used to play the game.

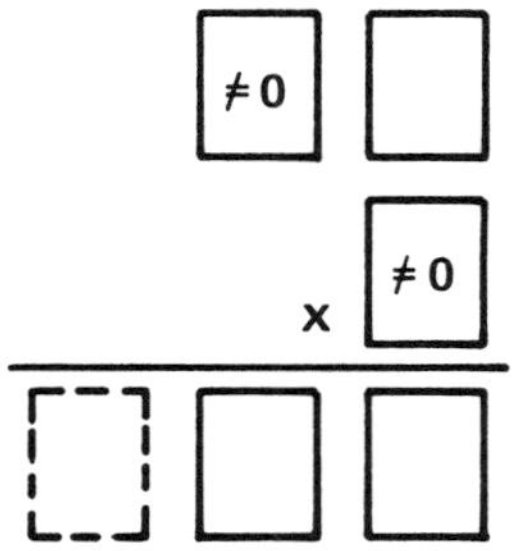

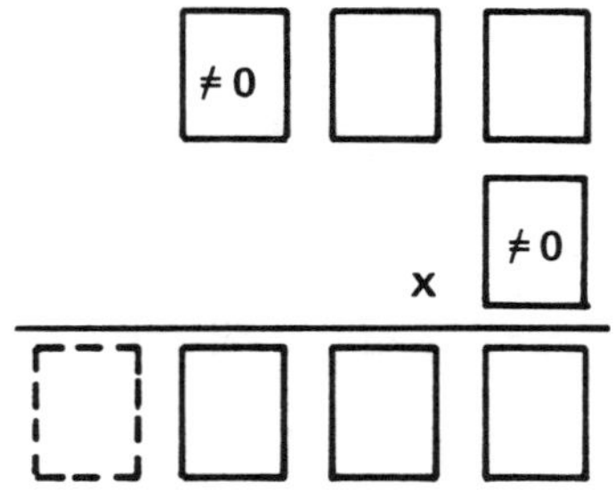

VARIATION 4: Build-A-Division-Problem

MAJOR CONCEPT: Division algorithm

NUMBER OF PLAYERS: Two or more

MATERIALS: Same as for Build-An-Addition-Problem

RULES: Build-A-Division-Problem is played in a similar way to Build-An-Addition-Problem, but it uses division. Either of the following division forms can be used to play the game.

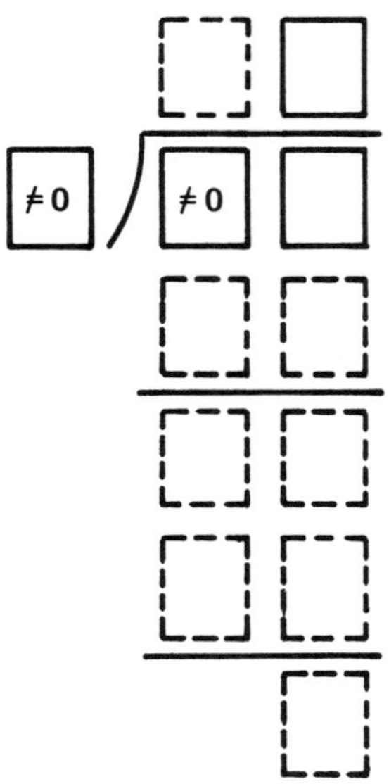

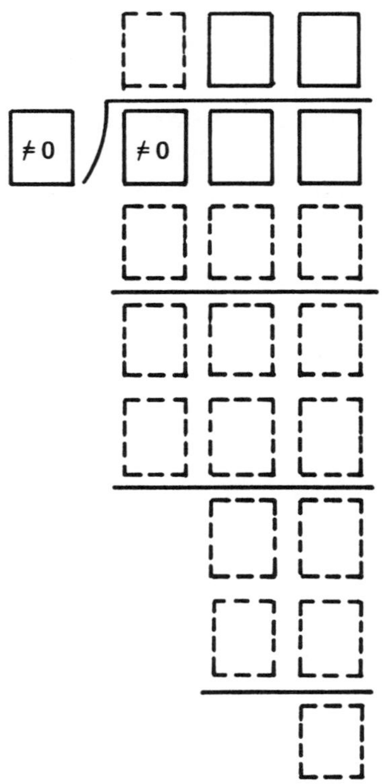

BUILD-AN-EXPRESSION

MAJOR CONCEPT: Simplifying expressions

NUMBER OF PLAYERS: Two or more

MATERIALS: 1. Paper and pencil for each player.

2. Four each of the following digit cards:

0	1	2	3	4	5	6	7	8	9

RULES: Each player copies this expression form:

$$(\square+\square)+(\square-\square)=8$$

The digit-deck is shuffled and placed face-up in the center of the table. The player to the left of the dealer copies the top-digit in one of her squares and then turns the top digit-card face-down beside the deck. Play continues until a player builds an expression that is equal to eight. The first player to do so wins the game and is awarded one point. If a player can not use the top digit she passes. If all players pass, the top digit-card is turned face-down and the first player who passed considers the next digit-card.

There are many expression forms that can be used. One way to vary the game is to prepare a duplicating master of different expression forms so a different one can be used for each game. Here are some other expression forms:

Game 1	$(\square+\square)+(\square-\square)=13$
Game 2	$(\square+\square)\times(\square\div\square)=24$
Game 3	$(\square+\square)\times(\square+\square)=36$
Game 4	$(\square\times\square)-(\square+\square)=20$
Game 5	$(\square-\square)\times(\square\div\square)=12$
Game 6	$(\square+\square)\div(\square-\square)=5$

ARITHMETIC TRADING

MAJOR CONCEPT: Computation algorithms

NUMBER OF PLAYERS: Four to six

MATERIALS: One set of eight exercise cards for each player in the game. All of the exercises of a set have the same answer.

Sample set for answer 54:

6 x 9	108 ÷ 2	100 − 46	31 + 23
28 + 26	65 − 11	72 − 18	2 x 27

Here is a set for 40:

2 x 20	80 ÷ 2	23 + 17	85 − 45
5 x 8	400 ÷ 10	4 x 10	20 + 20

If there are four players, there will be four of these sets making a deck of 32 cards. For five players there will be 40 cards (five sets of eight) and for six players there will be 48 cards (six sets of eight).

RULES: One player shuffles the cards and deals them one at a time, face-down, to the players. Each player will have eight cards to be sorted into sets according to the answer of the exercises. For example, a player holding these cards would sort them as shown.

54 set	40 set	62 set	60 set
6 x 9, 72 − 18, 100 − 46, 65 − 11	20 + 20, 5 x 8	37 + 25	100 − 40

The object of the game is to get all eight cards of the same set by trading cards, sight unseen, with the other players. The first player to complete a set is the winner.

To trade, each player selects from her hand some cards that she wishes to trade, holds them face-down in front of her, and calls out the number of cards until she finds someone who will exchange the same number of cards. For example, if a player wishes to trade three cards, she will hold the three cards in front of her, face-down, and call out, "Three. Three," until she finds someone who will trade three cards. After making a trade the player looks at her new cards, keeps those she wants, and then tries to arrange another trade. Players continue to trade in this way until a player collects all eight cards in one set. She shows her cards for the other players to check. If she has made no error, she is the winner.

A player is never forced to trade with another player and a player may change her mind about the number of cards she wishes to trade.

FRACTIONS MATCH

VARIATION 1: Equivalent Fractions Match

MAJOR CONCEPT: Equivalent fractions

NUMBER OF PLAYERS: Two to six

MATERIALS: Forty-nine cards – twelve groups of four cards each, and one unmatched card. Each group consists of four equivalent fractions.

$\frac{1}{2}$	$\frac{2}{4}$	$\frac{3}{6}$	$\frac{4}{8}$
$\frac{1}{3}$	$\frac{2}{6}$	$\frac{3}{9}$	$\frac{4}{12}$
$\frac{2}{3}$	$\frac{4}{6}$	$\frac{6}{9}$	$\frac{8}{12}$
$\frac{1}{4}$	$\frac{2}{8}$	$\frac{3}{12}$	$\frac{4}{16}$
$\frac{3}{4}$	$\frac{6}{8}$	$\frac{9}{12}$	$\frac{12}{16}$
$\frac{3}{2}$	$\frac{6}{4}$	$\frac{9}{6}$	$\frac{12}{8}$
$\frac{4}{3}$	$\frac{8}{6}$	$\frac{12}{9}$	$\frac{16}{12}$
$\frac{1}{5}$	$\frac{2}{10}$	$\frac{3}{15}$	$\frac{4}{20}$
$\frac{2}{5}$	$\frac{4}{10}$	$\frac{6}{15}$	$\frac{8}{20}$
$\frac{3}{5}$	$\frac{6}{10}$	$\frac{9}{15}$	$\frac{12}{20}$
$\frac{4}{5}$	$\frac{8}{10}$	$\frac{12}{15}$	$\frac{16}{20}$
$\frac{6}{5}$	$\frac{12}{10}$	$\frac{18}{15}$	$\frac{24}{20}$

The unmatched card:

RULES: This game is played in a similar way to the child's game *Old Maid*. The players sit in a circle. One player shuffles the cards and deals them one at a time, face-down, until all cards have been dealt. Each player discards pairs that match, that is, two cards showing equivalent fractions. For example, suppose a player has these three cards, among others, in his hand.

$\frac{1}{2}$	$\frac{3}{6}$	$\frac{4}{8}$

He can discard any two of them, but not all three since cards must be discarded in pairs. The cards are discarded face-up so that other players can check for errors. When this has been completed, each player has in his hand only unmatched cards.

Next, the dealer takes, without looking, one card from the hand of the player on his right. If that card matches a card in his hand, he pairs the two cards and discards the pair face-up in front of him. Then the player on the dealer's right takes one card from the player on his right and, if possible, pairs it with one in his own hand.

Play continues in this way around the circle to the right. As the cards move from player to player they will eventually all be paired and discarded – except for the unmatched card. When a player loses all of his cards, he is a winner and drops out of the play. The loser is the last player left, the one who last holds the odd card.

VARIATION 2: Equivalent Fractions Match

MAJOR CONCEPT: Equivalent Fractions – mixed numbers

NUMBER OF PLAYERS: Two to six.

MATERIALS: Twenty pairs of cards and one card with an empty square on it. One card of each pair shows an improper fraction and the other shows a mixed number.

Sample pairs:

$\frac{3}{2}$	$1\frac{1}{2}$
$\frac{8}{3}$	$2\frac{1}{3}$
$\frac{7}{4}$	$1\frac{3}{4}$

RULES: This game is played in a similar way to Equivalent Fractions Match.

VARIATION 3: Fractions and Regions Match

MAJOR CONCEPT: Relating fractions to parts of things

NUMBER OF PLAYERS: Two to six

MATERIALS: Twenty pairs of cards and one card with an empty square on it. One card of each pair shows a fraction and the other shows a square with that fraction of it shaded.

Sample pairs:

$\frac{1}{2}$ 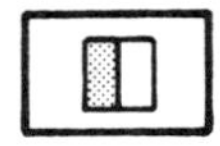

$\frac{2}{3}$ 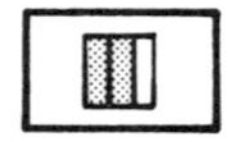

$\frac{3}{2}$ 

RULES: This game is played in a similar way to Equivalent Fractions Match.

VARIATION 4: Fraction - Decimal Match

MAJOR CONCEPT: Equivalence of fractions and decimals

NUMBER OF PLAYERS: Two to six

MATERIALS: Twenty pairs of cards and one card with an empty square on it. One of each pair has on it a common fraction and the other has on it the equivalent decimal fraction.

Sample pairs:

$\frac{1}{2}$	.5	$\frac{1}{4}$	.25
$\frac{3}{4}$	.75	$\frac{1}{5}$	.2
$\frac{3}{2}$	1.5	$\frac{7}{5}$	1.2

Do not use fractions like $\frac{1}{3}$ that do not have finite decimal equivalents.

RULES: This game is played in a similar way to Equivalent Fractions Match.

VARIATION 5: Fractions, Decimals, and Per Cents Match

MAJOR CONCEPT: Equivalence of fractions, decimals, and per cents

NUMBER OF PLAYERS: Two to six.

MATERIALS: One card with a square on it and forty cards in sets of four. Each set of four has two fractions, one decimal, and one per cent that are all equivalent.

Sample cards:

$\frac{1}{2}$	$\frac{2}{4}$	.5	50%
$\frac{1}{4}$	$\frac{2}{8}$	.25	25%

Use only fractions that have terminating decimal equivalents. For example, do not use $\frac{1}{3}$.

RULES: This game is played in a similar way to Equivalent Fractions Match.

VARIATION 6: Fractions and Per Cents Match

MAJOR CONCEPT: Equivalence of decimals and per cents

NUMBER OF PLAYERS: Two to six

MATERIALS: One card showing a square and twenty pairs of cards. One card of each pair shows a common fraction and the other shows the equivalent per cent.

Sample cards:

$\frac{1}{2}$	50%	$\frac{5}{4}$	125%
$\frac{1}{3}$	$33\frac{1}{3}$%	1	100%

RULES: This game is played in a similar way to Equivalent Fractions Match.

FRACTION FISHIN'

VARIATION 1: Fishin' for Equivalent Fractions

MAJOR CONCEPT: Matching equivalent fractions

NUMBER OF PLAYERS: Two to six

MATERIALS: Twelve sets of four cards showing equivalent fractions.

Sample set for $\frac{1}{2}$: $\frac{1}{2}$ $\frac{2}{4}$ $\frac{3}{6}$ $\frac{4}{8}$

Sample set for $\frac{2}{3}$: $\frac{2}{3}$ $\frac{4}{6}$ $\frac{6}{9}$ $\frac{8}{12}$

Sample set for $\frac{3}{2}$: $\frac{3}{2}$ $\frac{6}{4}$ $\frac{9}{6}$ $\frac{12}{8}$

RULES: One player shuffles the cards, deals five cards to each player, and places the rest of the deck face-down in the center of the table. Each player then discards pairs of matching cards, that is, pairs of cards from the same set. Each discarded pair is shown to the other players so they can check for errors. After all matching pairs have been discarded, play begins with the player to the left of the dealer and moves to the left. When it is her turn, a player asks the player on her right for a card with a specific number. For example, she may say, "Give me a $\frac{1}{2}$," or "Give me a $\frac{3}{4}$." If the player who is asked has such a card, she must give it to the player who asked for it. If the asked player does not have such a card, then the player who asked must take a card from the deck. In either case, if pairs are formed, they are shown and discarded. The first player to run out of cards is the winner. Two players may run out of cards on the same play and tie as winners.

VARIATION 2: Fractions and Regions Fishin'

MAJOR CONCEPT: Matching fractions and regions

NUMBER OF PLAYERS: Two to six

MATERIALS: Twenty-four pairs of cards. One card of each pair shows a fraction and the other shows a region with that fraction of it shaded.

Sample sets: $\frac{1}{2}$ $\frac{3}{2}$ $\frac{3}{4}$ $\frac{5}{4}$

A set of 24 fractions that could be used is, $\frac{1}{2}, \frac{3}{2}, \frac{1}{3}, \frac{2}{3}, \frac{4}{3}, \frac{5}{3}, \frac{1}{4}, \frac{3}{4}, \frac{5}{4}, \frac{7}{4}, \frac{1}{5}, \frac{2}{5}, \frac{3}{5}, \frac{4}{5}, \frac{6}{5}, \frac{7}{5}, \frac{1}{6}, \frac{5}{6}, \frac{7}{6}, \frac{1}{8}, \frac{3}{8}, \frac{5}{8}, \frac{7}{8}, \frac{9}{8}$.

RULES: This game is played in a similar way to Fishin' for Equivalent Fractions.

VARIATION 3: Fractions, Decimals, and Per Cents Fishin'

MAJOR CONCEPT: Equivalent fractions, decimals, and per cents

NUMBER OF PLAYERS: Two to six

MATERIALS: Twelve sets of four cards. In each set the four cards show equivalent fractions, per cents, and decimals.

Sample set for $\frac{1}{2}$:	$\frac{1}{2}$	$\frac{2}{4}$	.5	50%
Sample set for $\frac{1}{3}$:	$\frac{1}{3}$	$\frac{2}{6}$	$\frac{3}{9}$	$33\frac{1}{3}\%$
Sample set for $\frac{3}{2}$:	$\frac{3}{2}$	$1\frac{1}{2}$	1.5	150%

RULES: This game is played in a similar way to Fishin' for Equivalent Fractions.

FRACTION RUMMY

VARIATION 1: Equivalent Fractions Rummy

MAJOR CONCEPT: Matching equivalent fractions

NUMBER OF PLAYERS: Two to four

MATERIALS: Forty-eight cards — twelve groups of four cards. The four cards in each group show equivalent fractions:

$\frac{1}{2}$	$\frac{2}{4}$	$\frac{3}{6}$	$\frac{4}{8}$
$\frac{1}{3}$	$\frac{2}{6}$	$\frac{3}{9}$	$\frac{4}{12}$
$\frac{2}{3}$	$\frac{4}{6}$	$\frac{6}{9}$	$\frac{8}{12}$
$\frac{1}{4}$	$\frac{2}{8}$	$\frac{3}{12}$	$\frac{4}{16}$
$\frac{3}{4}$	$\frac{6}{8}$	$\frac{9}{12}$	$\frac{12}{16}$
$\frac{3}{2}$	$\frac{6}{4}$	$\frac{9}{6}$	$\frac{12}{8}$
$\frac{4}{3}$	$\frac{8}{6}$	$\frac{12}{9}$	$\frac{16}{12}$
$\frac{1}{5}$	$\frac{2}{10}$	$\frac{3}{15}$	$\frac{4}{20}$
$\frac{2}{5}$	$\frac{4}{10}$	$\frac{6}{15}$	$\frac{8}{20}$
$\frac{3}{5}$	$\frac{6}{10}$	$\frac{9}{15}$	$\frac{12}{20}$
$\frac{4}{5}$	$\frac{8}{10}$	$\frac{12}{15}$	$\frac{16}{20}$
$\frac{6}{5}$	$\frac{12}{10}$	$\frac{18}{15}$	$\frac{24}{20}$

RULES: The dealer shuffles the deck and deals seven cards to each player. The next card is turned face-up in the center of the table and the rest of the deck is stacked face-down next to it. Each player builds books of three or four matching cards from her hand. Matching cards are cards with equivalent fractions.

Sample books:

$\frac{1}{2}$ $\frac{4}{8}$ $\frac{2}{4}$

$\frac{1}{5}$ $\frac{2}{10}$ $\frac{3}{15}$ $\frac{4}{20}$

The play moves in a clockwise direction starting with the player on the dealer's left. When it is her turn, a player draws one card, either the top card of the deck or the top card of the discard pile. Then, if she has any books, she may lay them in front of her for everyone to see. If she has one card that matches a book that someone else has played, she may also display it face-up in front of her. Finally, the player must discard one card face-up on the top of the discard pile.

If all of the cards in the deck are used before a player goes out, the discard pile, except for the top card, can be shuffled and used as the deck.

Play ends when a player runs out of cards by discarding her last card. At this time, each player scores one point for each card she has laid down in front of her and loses one point for each card she still holds in her hand. Notice that the player who goes out scores seven points and the others score fewer points.

Next all of the cards are shuffled and dealt and play starts again. The game continues until one player scores a total of 50 or more points.

Note that a player is not required to display a book if she does not wish to. There are sometimes advantages to holding books for several hands and going out all at once.

VARIATION 2: Fractions, Decimals, and Per Cents Rummy

MAJOR CONCEPT: Equivalent fractions, decimals, and per cents

NUMBER OF PLAYERS: Two to four

MATERIALS: Twelve sets of four cards. Each set contains equivalent fractions, decimals, and per cents.

Sample set:

$\frac{1}{2}$ $\frac{50}{100}$ .5 50%

$\frac{1}{3}$ $\frac{9}{27}$ $\frac{5}{15}$ $33\frac{1}{3}\%$

RULES: This game is played in a similar manner to Equivalent Fractions Rummy.

BUILD–A–FRACTION

MAJOR CONCEPT: Equivalent fractions

NUMBER OF PLAYERS: Two or more

MATERIALS: 1. Four each of the following digit cards:

0 1 2 3 4 5 6 7 8 9

2. One each of the following fraction cards:

$\frac{0}{2}$ $\frac{1}{2}$ $\frac{2}{2}$ $\frac{3}{2}$ $\frac{4}{2}$ $\frac{5}{2}$

$\frac{0}{3}$ $\frac{1}{3}$ $\frac{2}{3}$ $\frac{3}{3}$ $\frac{4}{3}$ $\frac{5}{3}$ $\frac{6}{3}$ $\frac{7}{3}$

$\frac{0}{4}$ $\frac{1}{4}$ $\frac{2}{4}$ $\frac{3}{4}$ $\frac{4}{4}$ $\frac{5}{4}$ $\frac{6}{4}$ $\frac{7}{4}$ $\frac{8}{4}$

$\frac{0}{5}$ $\frac{1}{5}$ $\frac{2}{5}$ $\frac{3}{5}$ $\frac{4}{5}$ $\frac{5}{5}$ $\frac{6}{5}$

$\frac{0}{6}$ $\frac{1}{6}$ $\frac{2}{6}$ $\frac{3}{6}$ $\frac{4}{6}$ $\frac{5}{6}$ $\frac{6}{6}$ $\frac{7}{6}$ $\frac{8}{6}$ $\frac{9}{6}$

$\frac{0}{8}$ $\frac{1}{8}$ $\frac{2}{8}$ $\frac{3}{8}$ $\frac{4}{8}$ $\frac{5}{8}$ $\frac{6}{8}$ $\frac{7}{8}$ $\frac{8}{8}$ $\frac{9}{8}$

3. Paper and pencil for each player.

RULES: Each player draws on his paper a heavy bar like this:

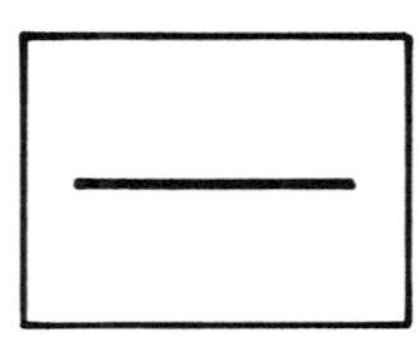

The dealer shuffles the digit-deck and deals five cards to each of the players. Each player places his five cards face-up in front of him. The fraction deck is shuffled and placed face-up in the center of the table.

To play the game, the first person to the left of the dealer uses the digit cards to build as many fractions as he can that are equivalent to the fraction on the top of the deck.

Example:

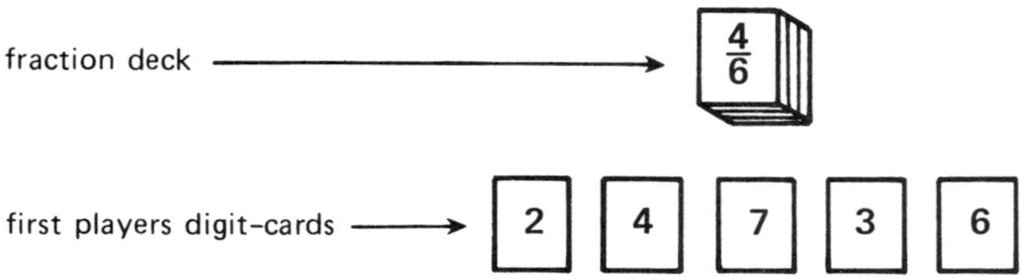

The first player could earn two points by building these two equivalent fractions:

If another player thinks that a mistake has been made, he should say "challenge." If the fraction *is* equivalent, the challenger loses a point. If not, he earns a point. Play proceeds in this manner until all players have played on the top fraction. Then the top card is turned face-down and play continues. The first player to get a predetermined number of points is the winner of the game. A reasonable number would be twelve.

Once a fraction is built, players can disassemble the fraction and use the same digit cards again to build another fraction. Also, the digit cards can be combined to build two and three digit numbers. For example:

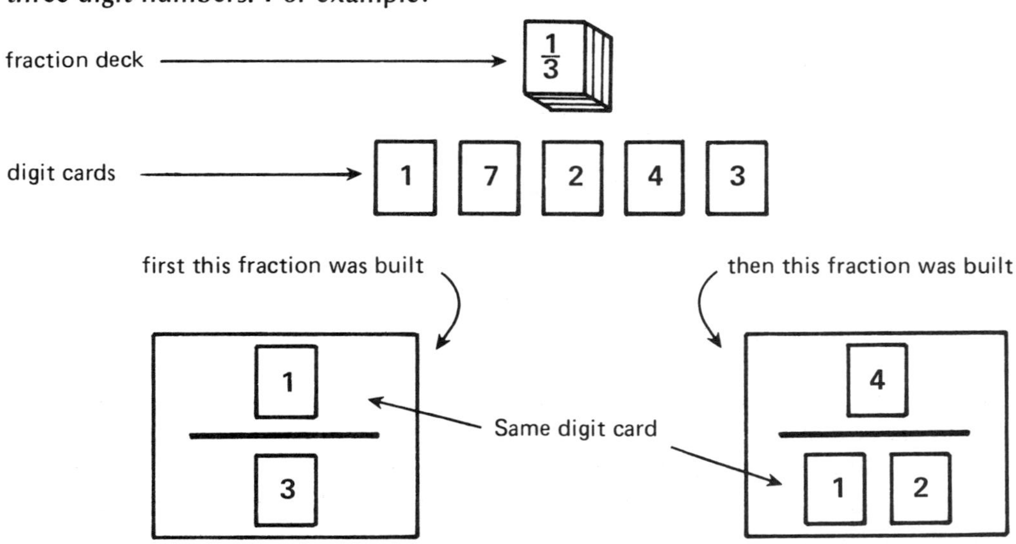

A variation of this game would be to turn down the top fraction-card after each player plays. Another would allow a challenger to earn a point by using an opponent's digit-cards to build an equivalent fraction that was overlooked.

BUILD–AN–ANSWER(Decimal)

VARIATION 1: Build-The-Greatest-Sum

MAJOR CONCEPT: Decimal algorithms

NUMBER OF PLAYERS: Two or more

MATERIALS: 1. Paper and pencil for each player

2. Four each of the following digit cards:

0 1 2 3 4 5 6 7 8 9

RULES: Each player copies this addition form:

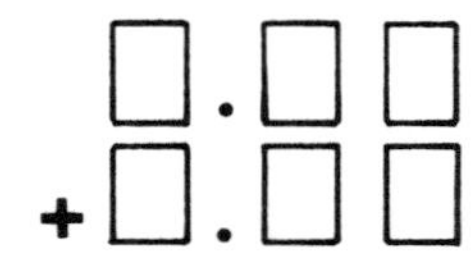

and places it face-up in front of her on the table. (This addition form could be prepared beforehand using a duplicating master.) A player shuffles the deck and places it, face-up, in the center of the table.

To play the game, the first person to the left of the player who shuffled, copies the top digit in any one of her six squares.

Sample:

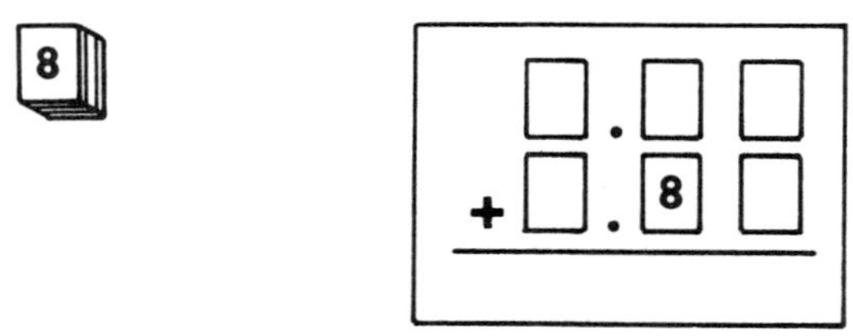

The other players should not see which square was filled in. Then she turns the top card face-down beside the deck. The next player copies the top digit in one of her squares and then turns the top card face-down. Play continues until all players have filled in all of their squares. If all the digit cards are used before all squares are filled in, the face-down deck should be turned over and play continued.

Each player computes her sum. The player having the greatest sum wins the game. The winner gets one point. The other players should always check the winner's addition.

One variation of the above game is Build-The-Least-Sum. In this game, the player who gets the least sum wins and is awarded one point. Other variations can be obtained by changing the addition form. Here are some other addition forms that can be used to play Build-The-Greatest-Sum or Build-The-Least-Sum.

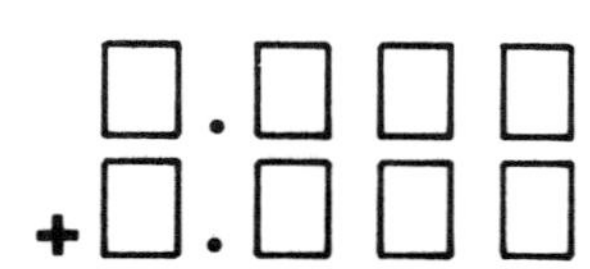

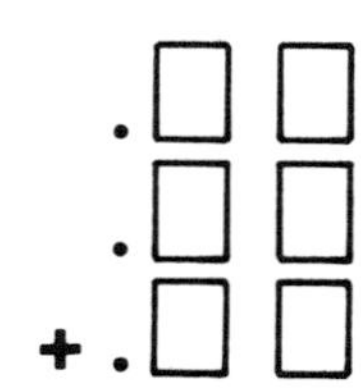

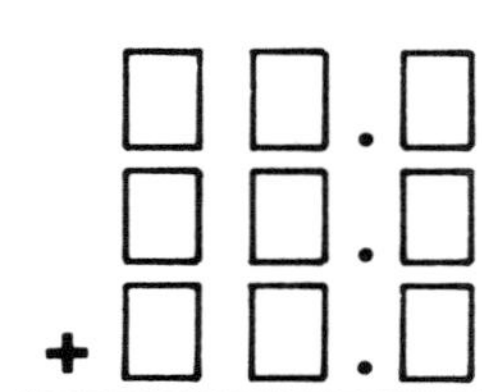

VARIATION 2: Build-The-Greatest-Difference

MAJOR CONCEPT: Subtraction algorithm

NUMBER OF PLAYERS: Two or more

MATERIALS: Same as in Build-The-Greatest-Sum

RULES: Build-The-Greatest-Difference is played in a similar way to Build-The-Greatest-Sum, using this subtraction form:

$$\begin{array}{r} \square.\square\,\square \\ -\,\square.\square\,\square \\ \hline \end{array}$$

It also has an additional rule: if a player fills her squares in such a way that the subtraction is impossible, she is disqualified from the game. For example, a player who filled her subtraction form like this:

$$\begin{array}{r} \boxed{5}.\boxed{8}\,\boxed{2} \\ -\,\boxed{7}.\boxed{3}\,\boxed{9} \\ \hline \end{array}$$

would be disqualified.

One variation of this game is Build-The-Least-Difference. Other variations can be obtained by changing the subtraction form. Here are some other subtraction forms:

$$\begin{array}{r} \square.\square\,\square\,\square \\ -\,\square.\square\,\square\,\square \\ \hline \end{array} \qquad \begin{array}{r} \square\,\square.\square\,\square\,\square \\ -\,\square\,\square.\square\,\square\,\square \\ \hline \end{array}$$

VARIATION 3: Build-The-Greatest-Product

MAJOR CONCEPT: Multiplication algorithm

NUMBER OF PLAYERS: Two or more

MATERIALS: Same as for Build-The-Greatest-Sum

RULES: Build-The-Greatest-Product is played in a similar way to Build-The-Greatest-Sum. It can be played with this multiplication form:

$$\begin{array}{r} \square.\square\,\square \\ \times\,\square \\ \hline \end{array}$$

The game can be varied by playing Build-The-Least-Product and by changing the multiplication form. Here are some other multiplication forms:

$$\begin{array}{r} \square.\square\,\square\,\square \\ \times\,.\square \\ \hline \end{array} \qquad \begin{array}{r} \square.\square\,\square \\ \times\,\square.\square \\ \hline \end{array}$$

VARIATION 4: Build-The-Greatest-Quotient

MAJOR CONCEPT: Division algorithm

NUMBER OF PLAYERS: Two or more

MATERIALS: Same as for Build-The-Greatest-Sum

RULES: Build-The-Greatest-Quotient is played in a similar way to Build-The-Greatest-Sum, using this division form:

□)□.□ □

It also has an additional rule: if a player fills her squares in such a way that the division is impossible, she is disqualified from the game. For example, a player who filled her squares like this: 0)4.7 2 would be disqualified.

The forms below could also be used to play Build-The-Greatest-Quotient or Build-The-Least-Quotient.

□)□.□ □ □　　　　□.□)□.□ □ □

FRACTION TRADING

MAJOR CONCEPT: Equivalent Fractions

NUMBER OF PLAYERS: Four to six

MATERIALS: One set of eight fraction cards for each player. All of the fractions in one set are equivalent.

Sample set for $\frac{1}{2}$:

$\frac{1}{2}$ $\frac{2}{4}$ $\frac{3}{6}$ $\frac{4}{8}$

$\frac{6}{12}$ $\frac{20}{40}$ $\frac{15}{30}$ $\frac{17}{34}$

Sample set for $\frac{3}{2}$:

$\frac{3}{2}$ $\frac{6}{4}$ $\frac{9}{6}$ $\frac{12}{8}$

$\frac{150}{100}$ $\frac{75}{50}$ $\frac{18}{12}$ $\frac{30}{20}$

Other sets of eight cards can be made for other rational numbers.

If there are four players, there will be four of these sets, making a deck of 32 cards. For five players there will be 40 cards (five sets of eight) and for six players there will be 48 cards (six sets of eight).

RULES: One player shuffles the cards and deals them one at a time, face-down, to the other players. Each player will have eight cards. Each player sorts his cards into sets of equivalent fractions.

Sample sorting:

$\frac{1}{2}$ $\frac{17}{34}$ $\frac{3}{6}$ $\frac{6}{12}$ — $\frac{1}{2}$ set

$\frac{4}{6}$ $\frac{6}{9}$ — $\frac{2}{3}$ set

$\frac{5}{6}$ — $\frac{5}{6}$ set

$\frac{12}{20}$ — $\frac{3}{5}$ set

The object of the game is to get all eight cards of the same set by trading cards, sight unseen, with the other players. The first player to complete a set is the winner.

To trade, each player selects from his hand some cards that he wishes to trade, holds them face-down in front of him, and calls out the number of cards until he finds someone who will exchange the same number of cards with him. For example, if a player wishes to trade three cards, he will hold the three cards in front of him, face-down, and call out, "Three. Three," until he finds someone who will trade three cards with him. After making a trade, the player keeps those he wants and then tries to arrange another trade. Players continue to trade in this way until a player collects all eight cards in one set. He shows his cards for the other players to check. If he has made no error, he is the winner.

A player is never forced to trade with another player, and he may change his mind about the number of cards he wishes to trade.

A variation of this game can be played by including decimal and per cent equivalents in some sets.

Sample set for $\frac{1}{2}$: | $\frac{1}{2}$ | | .5 | | 50% | | $\frac{50}{100}$ |

Also, mixed numerals can be included for rational numbers greater than one.

FRACTION CONCENTRATION

VARIATION 1: Equivalent Fractions Concentration

MAJOR CONCEPT: Equivalent fractions

NUMBER OF PLAYERS: Two to four

MATERIALS: Twenty cards in pairs as follows:

$\frac{1}{2}$	$\frac{1}{3}$	$\frac{2}{3}$	$\frac{1}{4}$	$\frac{3}{4}$
$\frac{2}{4}$	$\frac{3}{9}$	$\frac{4}{6}$	$\frac{3}{12}$	$\frac{15}{20}$
$\frac{1}{5}$	$\frac{3}{2}$	$\frac{4}{3}$	$\frac{2}{5}$	$\frac{1}{6}$
$\frac{2}{10}$	$\frac{6}{4}$	$\frac{12}{9}$	$\frac{6}{15}$	$\frac{2}{12}$

RULES: Shuffle the cards carefully and deal them face-down into four rows of five cards in each row.

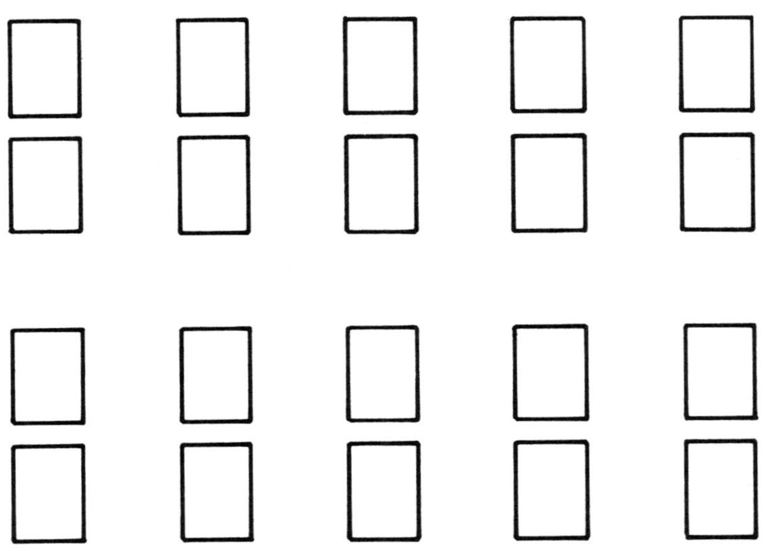

The player to the left of the dealer turns any two of the cards face-up in place. If the two cards show equivalent fractions, the player takes them. She then plays again. If the cards do not show equivalent fractions, they are turned, face-down, in the same places. The next player to the left then plays. The game ends when all of the cards have been paired. The winner is the player with the most pairs. Players who pay attention and remember the placements of the exposed cards have an advantage.

The deck of cards can be varied by changing some of the cards. For example, $\boxed{\frac{3}{6}}$ and $\boxed{\frac{7}{14}}$ for the number $\frac{1}{2}$. The number of cards used can be varied.

VARIATION 2: Fractions and Regions Concentration

MAJOR CONCEPT: Matching fractions and regions

NUMBER OF PLAYERS: Two to four

MATERIALS: Twenty cards in pairs. Each pair contains a fraction card and a region card.

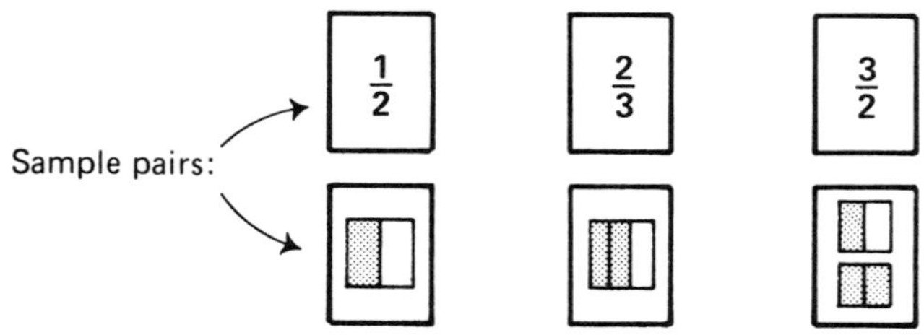

RULES: The game is played in a similar way to Equivalent Fractions Concentration.

VARIATION 3: Fractions and Decimals Concentration

MAJOR CONCEPT: Matching fractions and decimals

NUMBER OF PLAYERS: Two to four

MATERIALS: Twenty cards in pairs. Each pair contains one fraction card and one decimal card.

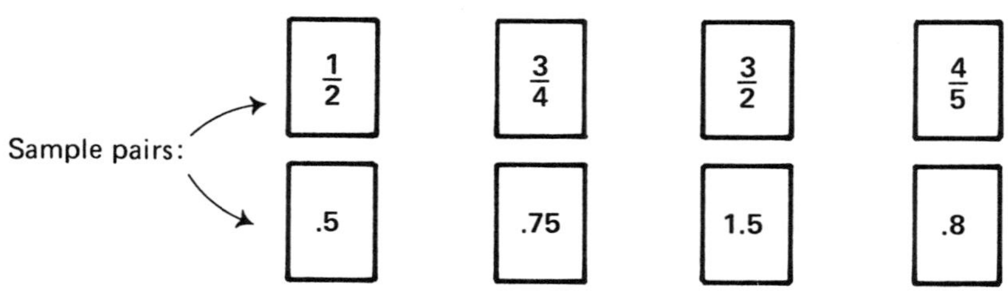

Use only fractions that have terminating decimal equivalents. For example, do not use $\boxed{\frac{1}{3}}$.

RULES: The game is played in a similar way to Equivalent Fractions Concentration.

VARIATION 4: Fractions and Per Cents Concentration

MAJOR CONCEPT: Matching equivalent fractions and per cents

NUMBER OF PLAYERS: Two to four

MATERIALS: Twenty cards in pairs. Each pair contains one fraction card and one per cent card.

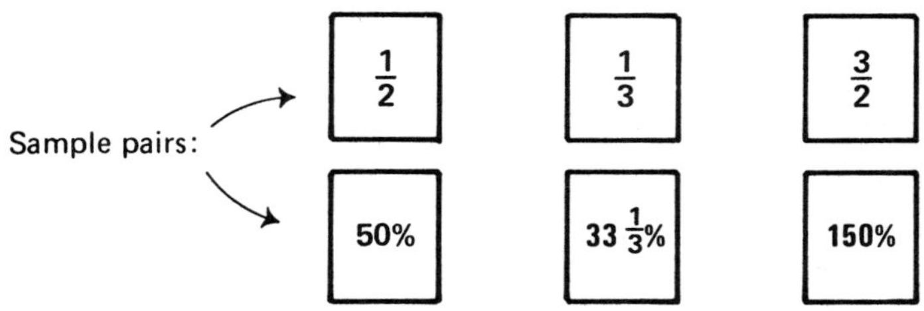

RULES: This game is played in a similar way to Equivalent Fractions Concentration.

MISCELLANEOUS GAMES

Many of the preceding games can be altered for practicing geometry skills. To save repetition, we shall describe suitable decks of cards and refer to earlier games for rules.

To practice vocabulary, a deck can be made of pairs of cards, one card of each pair showing a picture of a geometric figure and the other card showing the name of that figure. Pairs can be made of geometric terms appropriate to the class.

Sample pairs:

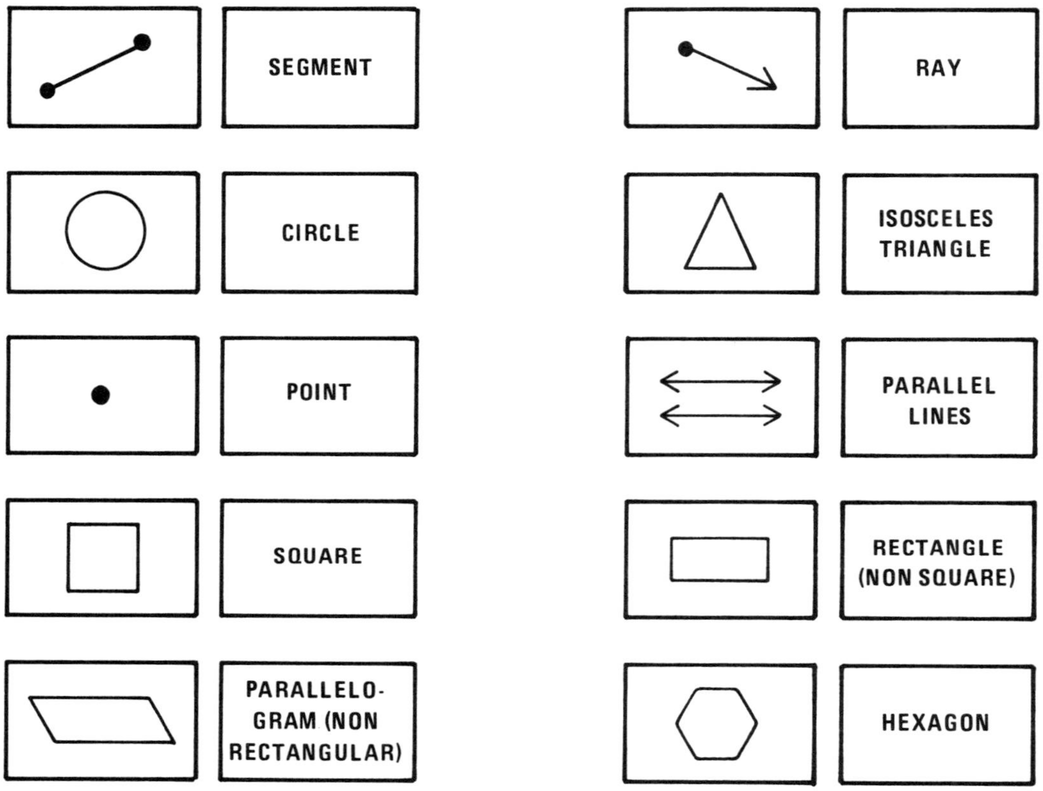

Note that since a square is also a rectangle, the picture of the square could be paired with the word *RECTANGLE*. Therefore, to eliminate this possibility, the word *NON-SQUARE* is also used.

To practice matching solid figures with their names, use pairs such as the following.

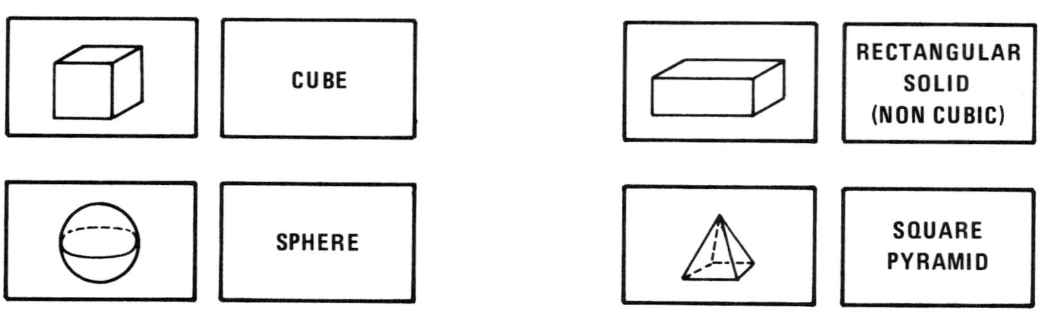

To provide practice matching congruent figures, another deck may be made of pairs of cards showing congruent figures. These cards are most easily made by cutting cardboard patterns of the figures and then tracing around the patterns. The patterns should be rotated, and sometimes flipped upside down, when tracing to make the second figure. Here are some examples:

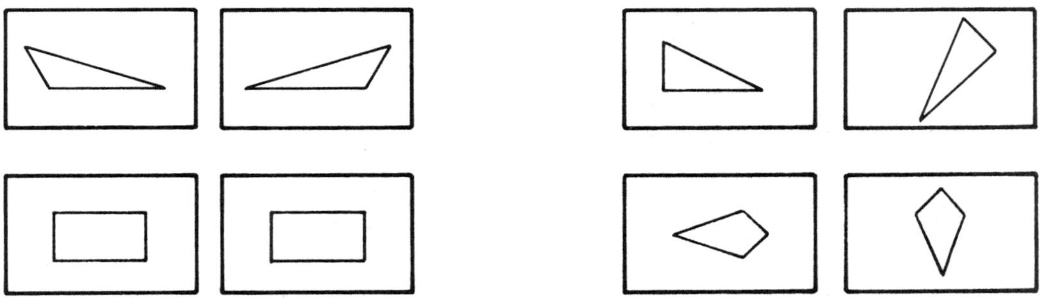

GAMES. With the appropriate number of pairs, the rules from the following games can be used.

1. Arithmetic Match (p.13). An unmatched card is also needed.
2. Arithmetic Concentration (p. 15)
3. Fishin' (p. 21)

ADD A—LENGTH

VARIATION 1: Inch-By-Inch

MAJOR CONCEPT: Linear measurement (U.S. Customary System)

NUMBER OF PLAYERS: Two or more

MATERIALS: 1. Yardstick

2. One marker, such as a pencil, a small triangle cut from paper, for each player.

3. One each of the following cards.

1 in.	$1\frac{1}{4}$ in.	$1\frac{1}{2}$ in.	$1\frac{3}{4}$ in.	2 in.	$2\frac{1}{2}$ in.	$2\frac{3}{4}$ in.	$\frac{1}{4}$ ft.	$3\frac{1}{4}$ in.
$3\frac{1}{2}$ in.	$\frac{1}{3}$ ft.	$4\frac{1}{4}$ in.	$4\frac{1}{2}$ in.	$4\frac{3}{4}$ in.	5 in.	$5\frac{1}{4}$ in.	$5\frac{1}{2}$ in.	
$\frac{1}{2}$ ft.	$6\frac{1}{4}$ in.	$6\frac{1}{2}$ in.	$6\frac{3}{4}$ in.	7 in.	$7\frac{1}{4}$ in.	$7\frac{1}{2}$ in.		
$7\frac{3}{4}$ in.	$\frac{2}{3}$ ft.	$8\frac{1}{4}$ in.	$8\frac{1}{2}$ in.	$8\frac{3}{4}$ in.	$\frac{1}{4}$ yd.	$9\frac{1}{4}$ in.	$9\frac{1}{2}$ in.	
$9\frac{3}{4}$ in.	$\frac{5}{6}$ ft.	$10\frac{1}{4}$ in.	$10\frac{1}{2}$ in.	$10\frac{3}{4}$ in.	11 in.	$11\frac{1}{4}$ in.	$11\frac{1}{2}$ in.	
$11\frac{3}{4}$ in.	$\frac{1}{3}$ yd.							

RULES: Tape the yardstick to the table top. One player shuffles the deck and places it face-down in the center of the table. Each player starts with her marker at the 0-point of the yardstick. The first player to the left of the shuffler turns the top card of the deck face-up and moves her marker along the yardstick the length indicated on the card. The next player turns up the next card and moves her marker the indicated length. Play continues in this manner until a player reaches the end of the yardstick. This player is the winner. If all the cards are used before anyone wins the game, the deck should be reshuffled and used again.

If a player makes a mistake that is noticed by another player, she must go back to the starting point. Some students have found it very useful to use two markers for each player, one to mark the starting point of a move and one to mark the ending point.

VARIATION 2: Centimeter-By-Centimeter

MAJOR CONCEPT: Linear measurement (Metric System)

NUMBER OF PLAYERS: Two or more

MATERIALS: 1. A meterstick

2. One marker, such as a pencil, a small triangle cut from paper, for each player.

3. One each of the following cards.

1 cm	2 cm	3 cm	4 cm	5 cm	6 cm	7 cm	8 cm
9 cm	1 dm	11 cm	1.2 dm	13 cm	14 cm	1.5 dm	16 cm
$\frac{1}{7}$ dm	18 cm	19 cm	2 dm	21 cm	2.2 dm	23 cm	24 dm
2.5 dm	26 cm	2.7 dm	28 cm	29 cm	3 dm		

RULES: This game is played in a similar way to Inch-By-Inch.

SHADE–A–REGION

VARIATION 1: Square-Inch-By-Square-Inch

MAJOR CONCEPT: Area (U.S. Customary System)

NUMBER OF PLAYERS: Two or more

MATERIALS:
1. A sheet of square inch graph paper, or dot paper, and pencil for each player.
2. One each of the following cards:

$\frac{1}{2}$ sq in	1 sq in	$1\frac{1}{2}$ sq in	2 sq in	$2\frac{1}{2}$ sq in	3 sq in	$3\frac{1}{2}$ sq in
4 sq in	$4\frac{1}{2}$ sq in	5 sq in	$5\frac{1}{2}$ sq in	6 sq in	$6\frac{1}{2}$ sq in	7 sq in
$7\frac{1}{2}$ sq in	8 sq in	$8\frac{1}{2}$ sq in	9 sq in	$9\frac{1}{2}$ sq in	10 sq in	$10\frac{1}{2}$ sq in
11 sq in	$11\frac{1}{2}$ sq in	12 sq in	$12\frac{1}{2}$ sq in	13 sq in	$13\frac{1}{2}$ sq in	14 sq in
$14\frac{1}{2}$ sq in	15 sq in					

RULES: Each player outlines an eight-inch by ten-inch rectangle on his paper. A player shuffles the deck and places it face-down in the center of the table. The player to his left turns over the top card and shades on his paper the area indicated on the card.

Sample: $3\frac{1}{2}$ sq in

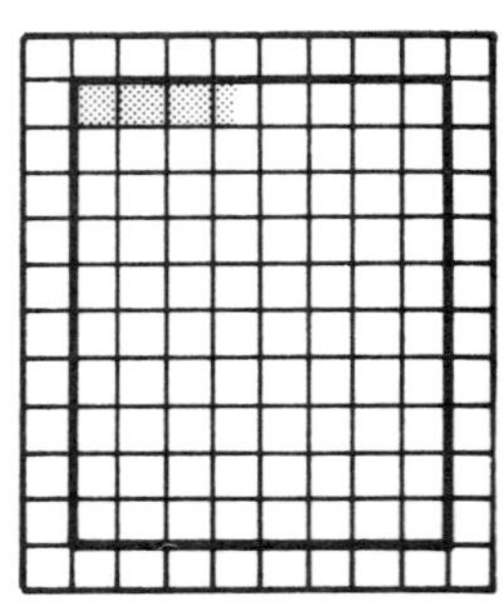

The next player turns over the next card and shades in the area designated. Play continues until a player has shaded in all of his eight-inch by ten-inch rectangle. The first player to do so, wins the game. If all the cards are used before a player wins, the face-down deck is shuffled and turned over and play continues.

VARIATION 2: Square Centimeter-By-Square Centimeter

MAJOR CONCEPT: Area (Metric System)

NUMBER OF PLAYERS: Two or more

MATERIALS: 1. A sheet of centimeter graph paper and a pencil for each player.

2. One each of the following cards.

$\frac{1}{2}$ sq cm	1 sq cm	$1\frac{1}{2}$ sq cm	2 sq cm	$2\frac{1}{2}$ sq cm	3 sq cm	$3\frac{1}{2}$ sq cm
4 sq cm	$4\frac{1}{2}$ sq cm	5 sq cm	$5\frac{1}{2}$ sq cm	6 sq cm	$6\frac{1}{2}$ sq cm	7 sq cm
$7\frac{1}{2}$ sq cm	8 sq cm	$8\frac{1}{2}$ sq cm	9 sq cm	$9\frac{1}{2}$ sq cm	10 sq cm	$10\frac{1}{2}$ sq cm
11 sq cm	$11\frac{1}{2}$ sq cm	12 sq cm	$12\frac{1}{2}$ sq cm	13 sq cm	$13\frac{1}{2}$ sq cm	14 sq cm
$14\frac{1}{2}$ sq cm	15 sq cm					

RULES: This game is played in a similar way to Square-Inch-By-Square-Inch.

POSITIVE AND NEGATIVE NUMBERS

Many of the preceding games can be adapted for practicing skills with positive and negative numbers. Again, to save repetition, we shall describe suitable decks of cards and refer to earlier games for rules.

MATERIALS: I. Two each of the following cards.

	−9	−8	−7	−6	−5	−4	−3	−2	−1
0	+1	+2	+3	+4	+5	+6	+7	+8	+9

GAMES: Using these cards students can play:

1. War (p. 12)
2. Addition War (p. 20)
3. Multiplication War (p. 20)

Students could also play Subtraction War. However, since the order of subtracting is usually important, one of two extra rules are needed. Either players must subtract in the order in which the cards are drawn (subtract the second from the first), or, they may subtract in whichever order gives them the greater difference.

4. Target Number (p. 51) Care must be taken to choose reasonable target numbers.
5. Build-An-Expression (p. 60)
6. Right on the Nose (p. 45)
7. Equations Rummy (p. 48)

II. Sets of eight cards of expressions with positive and negative numbers.

Sample set for -12:

$^{-}3 \times {}^{+}4$	$^{+}6 \times {}^{-}2$	$^{+}2 - {}^{-}14$	$^{-}7 + {}^{-}5$
$^{-}14 - {}^{-}2$	$^{+}24 \div {}^{-}2$	$^{-}15 + {}^{+}3$	$^{-}5 - {}^{+}7$

Arithmetic Trading (p. 61) can be played with these cards.

